Sarbanes-Oxley
Simplified

Sarbanes-Oxley Simplified

Michel Morley, CPA

Nixon-Carre Ltd., Toronto, ON

Library and Archives Canada Cataloguing in Publication

Morley, Michel, 1952-
      Sarbanes-Oxley Simplified / Michel Morley.

ISBN 0-9737470-3-X

     1. United States. Sarbanes-Oxley Act of 2002.
2. Corporations--Accounting--Law and legislation--United States. 3. Disclosure of information--Law and legislation--United States. 4. Corporate governance--Law and legislation--United States. I. Title.

KF1446.A31M67 2005   346.73'0664
C2005-903601-X

Distributed by:

Nixon-Carre Ltd.
P.O. Box 92533
Carlton RPO
Toronto, Ontario, M5A 4N9

To order: (416) 929-1202
www.nixon-carre.com

Printed and bound in Canada

Contents

Chapter 6 cont.
    Analyst Conflicts of Interest
    Time Limitations
    Conflicts of Interest by Securities Analysts

Section 3 - Implementing The Act

    Financial Controls: The Backbone of Risk Management
    Starting At the Top
    A Simple Model
    Assessment of the Risk of Misstatement
    Mapping the Process
    Using Qualitative and Quantitative Methods
    Establishing a Risk Management Plan
    Monitoring and Feedback
    Maintaining Compliance

    IT: Documentation for Compliance
    IT Crosses All Boundaries
    Controls for Sensitive Information
    Electronic Approvals
    Controls for Hardware and Software
    Network Administration
    Backup
    Safeguarding Personal Information

    Risk of Manipulation
    Determining Accountability for Inventory
    Inventory Obsolescence
    Inventory Valuation
    A Sale That Is Not a Sale
    Inventory Counts

Chapter 12 cont.
Customer Deposits
Asset Securitization
Marketable Securities
Assets and Expenses

Bill 198 and Sarbanes-Oxley
Material Changes Must Be Reported Immediately
Penalties
Fraud and Market Manipulation
Investors Can Sue Directors and Officers
Time Limits
Disclosures
Pro-forma Information
Audit Committees
Internal Controls
Similar Key Provisions
Similar Compliance Procedures
Around The World

Is it accurate? Are you sure? Can you prove it?
Internal Reports: Decision Tools
Additional Focus on Off-Balance-Sheet Transactions
Foreign Company Internal Reporting
Sarbanes-Oxley Compliance Software
Documentation
Internal Controls to Manage Risk
Who Approves Reporting?
Internal Reporting Becomes External Reporting
Role of the Auditor - Year End and Ongoing Process
Living with Sarbanes-Oxley

Mike Morley can be reached by phone at

416-275-1278

or by email at **mikemorley@sympatico.ca**.

www.mikemorley.com

Introduction

A Simple Solution To A Complex Problem

Sarbanes-Oxley is a US law that came into effect July 30, 2002 to strengthen corporate governance and restore investor confidence. Sponsored by Maryland Senator Paul Sarbanes and Ohio Congressman Michael Oxley, the Act is intended to provide a strong deterrent to those individuals who might be tempted to manipulate corporate financial data for their own gain. The penalties imposed by the Act include substantial fines and significant prison terms.

Ignorance is no longer an excuse. The Act makes CEO's and CFO's personally responsible not only for financial statements that accurately reflect the financial condition of the company, but also makes them responsible for setting up and maintaining systems that ensure that they actually know the truth about what is going on in the company. This requirement is a brilliantly simple solution to the ever present problem of fraud.

Some additional features of the Act include legislation intended to prevent conflict of interest between auditors and the companies that they are auditing, protection for employees of publicly traded companies who provide evidence of fraud, and new Statutes of Limitations for securities fraud.

Foreign subsidiaries of US companies are also required to comply with this US law. Many other countries have created or are in the process of creating similar legislation due to its effectiveness.

Although the Sarbanes-Oxley Act of 2002 was intended to restore investor confidence in the audited financial statements of public companies, the practice of establishing and continually evaluating financial controls is equally beneficial to private companies and their creditors.

This book demystifies the implementation process.

The Birth of Sarbanes-Oxley   1

In the past, investors and lenders trusted executives of large, reputable public companies, investment banks, credit rating agencies, and, most of all, large auditing firms, to provide them with accurate financial information on which to make sound investing and lending decisions. Unfortunately, as we now know, many of these players traded their principles for money. Many had been profiting from unethical, if not downright illegal, practices for some time before Enron came crashing down. The collapse of Enron made it impossible for the US government to continue to ignore what was going on. Legislators were forced to take action in order to earn back the trust of investors.

The Sarbanes-Oxley Act of 2002 is a US law that came into effect July 30, 2002 to strengthen corporate governance and restore investor confidence. Sponsored by Maryland Senator Paul Sarbanes and Ohio Congressman Michael Oxley, the goal of the Act is to protect investors by improving the accuracy and reliability of corporate disclosures.

The Sarbanes-Oxley Act of 2002 was enacted mainly as a response to the largest bankruptcy in United States history (Enron).

Before Sarbanes-Oxley

Prior to the scandals that precipitated the Sarbanes-Oxley Act of 2002, investors and creditors trusted that the process of auditing financial statements would detect any material misstatement. Investors and creditors relied on a public company's audited financial statements to make investment and lending decisions.

Enron: The Destruction of Investor Confidence

The largest corporate bankruptcy in US history (Enron) shook the very foundation upon which the securities exchange system was founded. The report card that investors and lenders used to make their decisions, the audited financial statement, could no longer be trusted. Investors and lenders lost confidence in public company senior management to tell them the truth.

Investors had trusted the accounting firm of Arthur Andersen, LLP, Enron's auditor, to be their "watchdog." However, Arthur Andersen, LLP, was receiving significant consulting contract revenue from Enron, in addition to being their auditing firm. SEC Investigators ultimately concluded that this conflict of interest contributed in large part to Arthur Andersen, LLP's, decision not to disclose Enron's contingent liability arising out of certain loan guarantees. The companies whose loans they were guaranteeing were "Special Purpose Entities" (SPE) that happened to be owned by Enron's CFO.

Special Purpose Entities

An SPE is a legal entity created by another entity (a sponsor) to carry out a specified purpose or activity. An SPE is often a financing vehicle that allows a sponsor entity to transfer assets to the SPE in exchange for cash, including "prepay transactions", which are transactions that involve a contract for a service or product to be delivered at a later date. In other words, the SPE would borrow money to "sell" a service or product and recognize the revenue although the service had not yet been delivered.

Off-Balance-Sheet Items

Section 401 of the Act stipulates that off-balance-sheet transactions must be disclosed. In Enron's case, because these loans were recorded on the SPE's balance sheet instead of Enron's, Enron appeared to be less debt ridden than it actually was, although it was still liable if the SPE defaulted on the loan. Enron used the lack of disclosure to hide the real indebtedness of the company.

In order for the scheme to work, the investment banks that provided the loans to the SPE's had to keep quiet, and they did. The investment banks were related to the credit rating agencies that gave Enron a good rating right up to four days before its bankruptcy. As a result of this complicity on the part of all the players involved, investors no longer trusted the companies, the auditors, the investment banks, and the credit rating agencies.

Enron was by no means the only company whose questionable accounting practices illustrated the need for stronger regulations. Before Enron, especially in the high tech bubble of the 1990's, there was an ever-growing pressure for companies to continually "beat expectations." Expectations were met and exceeded, even if it meant manipulating financial data. In addition, because stock options were a large part of executive compensation packages, manipulating financial information to produce increasing stock prices proved too tempting for some executives who became millionaires almost overnight.

Revenue Recognition

In order for public companies to continue "beating expectations" and keep the stock price going up, (which allowed executives to collect big bonuses), one of the techniques they used was to manipultate the "timing" of revenue. Revenue recognition is supposed to be based on GAAP (Generally Accepted Accounting Principles).

Conservatism is one of the GAAP principles. It says that, when in doubt, do not recognize the revenue until you are sure. Unfortunately, some public companies anticipated recognition of revenue by including it in their current period instead of waiting for the evidence that revenue had actually been earned. As well, some companies received asset-financing money but classified it as revenue, although there was no evidence to support this accounting treatment.

Investors Betrayed

Investors felt betrayed by the accountants and auditors they had depended upon to be the gatekeepers. Auditors were supposed to be disinterested third parties who could be relied upon to ring the alarm if something was not right. Investors and lenders were let down also by the investment banks and the credit rating agencies whose expertise was never in question. The lack of confidence in the established financial reporting system threatened the ability of public companies to obtain equity financing from public securities exchanges.

Lack of Public Confidence

This lack of confidence in public company financial statements was a crisis that could not be allowed to continue. Investors were withdrawing in large numbers from the rapidly declining markets until they could see what would happen next.

Lenders were scrambling to reassess their positions. While trying to protect their investments, they were reluctant to lend money to public companies based on audited financial statements. The outlook for public companies that needed financing became bleak.

Politically, the U.S. government had to stabilize the situation and restore investor confidence. The Sarbanes-Oxley Act of 2002 was drawn up to entice investors and lenders back into the markets. These dollars are needed to run large public companies. The Act has far reaching effects, well beyond the boardrooms of worldwide corporate head offices, public audit firms, investment banks, and credit rating agencies.

The Act is intended to provide a strong deterrent to those players who might be tempted to manipulate financial data for their own gain, including company executives, employees, auditors, investment banks and credit rating agencies.

Ignorance Is No Longer An Excuse

The penalties imposed by the Act include substantial fines and significant prison terms. Depending on the circumstances, they can be as high as $5 million in fines, in addition to any profits from selling shares, and up to 25 years in prison.

Bernard Ebbers, the former CEO of WorldCom, was found guilty on nine counts in an $11 billion accounting fraud. At this writing, he awaits sentencing, and faces up to 85 years in prison. Ebbers, a former milkman, basketball coach and Best Western hotel owner, said he was unaware of the fraud.

Kenneth Lay, former CEO of Enron, is set to have his trial begin in early 2006. Facing 175 years in prison and severe fines if found guilty, Lay also claims that he knew nothing of the fraud at his company.

A Simple Solution

The Sarbanes-Oxley Act of 2002 is a brilliant and simple solution to the "I didn't know" defence. It makes CEO's and CFO's personally responsible not only for financial statements that accurately reflect the financial condition of the company, but also makes CEO's and CFO's personally responsible for setting up and maintaining systems that ensure that they know. In other words, the Act says that CEO's and CFO's must ensure that they know everything that they ought to know. For CEO's and CFO's, ignorance of what is going on in their company is no longer an excuse.

Three Questions

It takes 66 pages to do so, but in effect, The Sarbanes-Oxley Act of 2002 asks three simple questions that CEO's and CFO's must answer:

1) Is it accurate?

Are the financial statements free of any material

misstatements so that they reflect the true financial condition of the company and can be relied upon by investors?

2) Are you sure?

CEO's and CFO's must certify that the internal financial controls of their companies work to the extent that they are informed about everything that should know. In addition, they must determine if any of the procedures in place pose a significant risk of producing inaccurate or incomplete financial information and show how they have taken steps to eliminate that risk.

3) Can you prove it?

CEO's and CFO's need to have documentation that satisfies the auditors and the SEC that their companies are doing what they say they are doing.

Not Just For Publicly Traded Companies

While the financial controls imposed by the Sarbanes-Oxley Act of 2002 are a legal obligation for publicly traded companies, they also serve as an excellent guide for growing private companies. Although the intention of the Act was to restore investor confidence in the audited financial statements of public companies, the practice of establishing and continually evaluating financial controls is equally beneficial to private companies. In particular, the creditors of private companies will benefit from financial statements that reflect more closely the financial condition of the company. They will feel more confident in assessing the company's ongoing ability to meet its covenants as required by the loan agreement.

When companies expand to the point beyond which a single person can run everything, they need control systems in place to manage operations. As they grow larger, these control systems need to become more sophisticated to adapt to the changing circumstances in the growing company.

Document Structure

The Sarbanes-Oxley Act of 2002 is divided into 11 chapters, or Titles, preceded by a table of contents and a list of definitions, with each section starting with the title number. For example, Section 802 is the second item in Title 8.

Chapter 1 Summary

• The Sarbanes-Oxley Act of 2002 is a US law that came into effect July 30, 2002 to strengthen corporate governance and restore investor confidence.

• The Act was enacted mainly as a response to the largest bankruptcy in United States history (Enron).

• Undisclosed off-balance-sheet items made Enron appear to be less debt ridden than it actually was. Enron used this lack of disclosure to hide the real indebtedness of the company.

• Enron was not the only company manipulating their financial data to manipulate the stock price. Revenue recognition issues including the "timing" of revenue and classifying asset-financing money as revenue were some of the problems that needed to be addressed.

• Conflicts of interest and collusion between auditors, analysts, senior management, and credit rating agencies resulted in investors being mislead about many companies' true financial situations.

• Ignorance is no longer an excuse, the Act makes CEO's and CFO's personally responsible not only for financial statements that accurately reflect the financial condition of the company, but also makes CEO's and CFO's personally responsible for setting up and maintaining systems that ensure that they know.

Regulatory Bodies

The Sarbanes-Oxley Act of 2002 establishes a new structure for regulating how public auditing firms audit public companies. The Securities and Exchange Commission, through the Public Company Accounting Oversight Board, oversees public auditing firms and their relationships with public companies.

TITLE I - The Public Company Accounting Oversight Board

The Public Company Accounting Oversight Board, made up of five members appointed by the Securities and Exchange Commission, reports directly to the Securities and Exchange Commission (who in turn reports to the federal government).

The Board's Mandate

The Public Company Accounting Oversight Board's mandate is to protect the interests of investors and the public by making sure that audits of public companies follow the securities laws and that audit reports are informative, accurate, and independent.

The Board's Functions

The Public Company Accounting Oversight Board's duties include:

- Registering public accounting firms
- Establishing standards of ethics and independence
- Inspecting registered public accounting firms
- Imposing sanctions

Public Company Accounting Oversight Board Membership

The Public Company Accounting Oversight Board has five members. It is interesting to note that only two members can be Certified Public Accountants. If one of those two members is the chairperson, he or she is not allowed to have practiced as a Certified Public Accountant for at least five years prior to his or her appointment to the Public Company Accounting Oversight Board. The thought is that this will make the chairperson more objective and less likely to be influenced by any public company they may have done work for in the past.

While serving on the Board, members cannot be employed by anyone else, or share in any of the profits of, or receive payments from, a public accounting firm. Members serve for five years and are limited to two terms, regardless of whether the terms are consecutive or not.

Mandatory Registration

The Sarbanes-Oxley Act of 2002 prohibits any firm or person other than a registered public accounting firm from participating in the preparation of any public company audit report.

Other than proprietary information, the Board makes available for public inspection information supplied by registered firms such as:

- The names of audit clients for the current and past year

- Annual fees from each client for audit services, other accounting services, and non-audit services

- Financial information for the recently completed fiscal year

- Quality control policies of the audit firm

- A list of all accountants (and their individual license or certification number) associated with the firm who contribute to audit reports

- The State license numbers of the firm itself

• Any pending criminal, civil, or administrative actions or disciplinary proceedings

• Any accounting disagreements between the issuer and the firm filed with the Securities and Exchange Commission (The public disclosure of these disagreements is intended to draw the attention of investors to any potential conflict of interest. It can also serve to alert the SEC of misconduct by auditing firms.)

• Auditing, quality control, and independence standards and rules

Keeping Auditing Records For 7 Years

Section 103 of the Act requires registered public accounting firms to keep audit work papers, and other information related to any audit report, for seven years. The scope as well as the results of the auditor's testing of the internal control structure and procedures, including material weaknesses in internal controls and any material noncompliance, must be recorded and kept for the same period. A second partner in the firm who was not in charge of the audit must also review every audit.

In addition, the auditor has to attest as to the adequacy of the public company's internal control procedures and make sure that detailed records are kept. They must "...*accurately and fairly reflect the transactions and dispositions of the assets.*" (Sarbanes-Oxley Act of

2002, p. 12.)

In other words, the auditor must provide reasonable assurance that generally accepted accounting principles were followed and that receipts and expenditures were approved by management.

Quality Control and Independence

In order to ensure the auditor's independence, the Sarbanes-Oxley Act of 2002 requires registered public accounting firms to uphold professional ethics and maintain independence from their audit clients and yet, in order to provide quality audit services, the public accounting firm must be intimately familiar with their client's business. For example, the auditor needs to be aware of audit issues, such as timing of revenue recognition or amounts of reserves, as they come up. Unfortunately, the need to "stay in the loop" needs to be balanced with the need for the audit firm to remain independent.

This is a tough balancing act that the firm needs to maintain. If the client insists on not following the audit firm's recommendations, the audit firm needs to examine the question and decide if they can continue being the company's auditor.

Auditing and Consulting

When auditing firms are offered consulting

opportunities, they must decide between auditing and consulting. If they decide to accept and continue the auditing engagement, they must forego the consulting revenue.

In addition to supervising audits and carrying out internal inspections, audit firms must specifically instruct their employees who deal with clients that they must behave in an ethical manner and maintain their independence at all times. Although the Act does not specifically forbid it, auditors should never take gifts form their clients or allow their clients to pay them inflated fees.

Inspections of Registered Public Accounting Firms

Regular Inspections

The Sarbanes-Oxley Act of 2002 calls for registered public accounting firms that issue more than 100 public company audits per year to be inspected by the Public Company Accounting Oversight Board every year. Those that prepare less than 100 are to be inspected at least every three years.

Regular inspections try to uncover any act or omission by a registered public accounting firm that may be in violation of The Sarbanes-Oxley Act of 2002, the rules of the Public Company Accounting Oversight Board and of the Securities and Exchange Commission. In addition, inspectors will look for violations of professional standards and of the auditing firm's own quality control policies.

Limited Publication of Inspection Reports

Although inspection reports are to be made available to the public, defects in the quality control systems of the auditing firm under inspection, if corrected within 12 months, will not appear in the inspection report when it is made public. For example, if the auditing firm issues an unqualified opinion for an audit client only to discover later that the audit did not catch a material misstatement, it must not only take immediate corrective action to resolve the problem, the audit firm needs to implement changes in its quality control systems to prevent this situation from happening again. If it satisfies the Public Company Accounting Oversight Board within 12 months that it has resolved the issue and corrected its internal quality control systems to prevent future occurrences, then the "defect" will not be made public.

Investigations and Disciplinary Proceedings

The Board has sweeping powers to investigate any suspected violation of any provision of:

- The Sarbanes-Oxley Act of 2002
- The rules of the Public Company Accounting Oversight Board
- The provisions of the securities laws relating to

the preparation and issuance of audit reports
- The obligations and liabilities of accountants preparing audit reports
- Breaches of professional standards

Gathering Evidence From Public Accounting Firms

The Public Company Accounting Oversight Board can subpoena the testimony and working papers (and any other document or information) of any accountant, accounting firm, or public company. The Board can revoke or suspend the accounting firm's and the individual accountant's registration if the firm or employee does not cooperate. In addition, the Board has the power to have the accountant's employment with the accounting firm terminated for not cooperating.

Sanctions

The Public Company Accounting Oversight Board can impose sanctions. Depending on the results of its investigation, it can:

- Censure (reprimand)
- Require additional professional education or training
- Fine a person up to of $100,000 per instance
- Fine a firm up to $2 million per instance (Sarbanes-Oxley Act of 2002, p. 18.)

If the Board finds "*intentional or repeated instances*

of negligent conduct", it can:

- Temporarily suspend or permanently revoke registration
- Limit activities of an accountant or firm
- Bar someone from working with any registered public accounting firm
- Fine a person up to of $750,000 per instance
- Fine a firm up to $15 million per instance. (Sarbanes-Oxley Act of 2002, p. 18.)

The Securities and Exchange Commission has the final say with regard to any rulings, such as sanctions that may be imposed by the Public Company Accounting Oversight Board.

Foreign Public Accounting Firms

A foreign public accounting firm is "*a public accounting firm that is organized and operates under the laws of a foreign government.*" (Sarbanes-Oxley Act of 2002, p. 20.)

Any foreign public accounting firm that prepares an audit report of a public company is subject to the same rules as a U.S. public accounting firm, even if the foreign public accounting firm does not actually issue audit reports but still has a significant part in the preparation of the audit reports.

If a U.S. public accounting firm relies on the

opinion of a foreign public accounting firm, the Sarbanes-Oxley Act of 2002 requires that the foreign public accounting firms agree to supply audit working papers to the Public Company Accounting Oversight Board or the Commission upon request.

TITLE VI - Commission Resources and Authority

Dealing With Improper Conduct

The Sarbanes-Oxley Act of 2002 characterizes improper professional conduct as either intentional or negligent.

Intentional or reckless conduct that results in a violation of applicable professional standards can be either a single instance of highly unreasonable conduct that occurred while the registered public accounting firm knew that heightened scrutiny was warranted, or it can be repeated instances of unreasonable conduct that indicates a lack of competence to practice. In other words, it will be considered intentional if it was serious and covered up, and will be considered negligent if it was done repeatedly because the auditor did not know any better.

The Securities and Exchange Commission has the power to limit or take away an individual's right to practice in their field if the Commission concludes that the person is guilty of the following:

- Not possessing the requisite qualifications to represent others
- To be lacking in character or integrity
- To have engaged in unethical or improper professional conduct
- To have willfully violated any provision of the securities laws

Penny Stock

Penny stock is stock that trades for less than $1 a share, although heavy promotion may lift prices temporarily higher. Most are traded OTC (Over the Counter). They are generally considered extremely speculative investments.

If someone dealing in penny stock is guilty of misconduct the court may temporarily or permanently prohibit that person from participating in any offering of penny stock. The court is particularly vigilant when it comes to penny stock because its speculative nature lends itself more easily to abuse.

Rules for Brokers, Dealers and Investment Advisors

Brokers, dealers and investment advisors can be barred or suspended by the Securities and Exchange Commission. They are subject to the same rules as those that govern banks. These rules can bar a person from the business of securities, banking, etc. because of fraudulent, manipulative, or deceptive conduct.

Chapter 2 Summary

• The Public Company Accounting Oversight Board's mandate is to protect the interests of investors and the public by making sure that audits of public companies follow the securities laws and that audit reports are informative, accurate, and independent.

• The Act prohibits any firm or person other than a registered public accounting firm from participating in the preparation of any public company audit report.

• Registered public accounting firms must keep audit work papers, and other information related to any audit report, for seven years. A second partner in the firm who was not in charge of the audit must also review every audit.

• When auditing firms are offered consulting opportunities, they must decide between auditing and consulting. If they accept the auditing engagement, they must forego the consulting revenue.

• Any foreign public accounting firm that prepares an audit report of a US public company is subject to the same rules as a U.S. public accounting firm.

• Regular inspections of registered public accounting firms by the Public Company Accounting Oversight Board is an attempt to uncover any act or omission that may be in violation of Act.

Corporate Responsibilities 3

The Sarbanes-Oxley Act of 2002 makes Public Company executives personally accountable by having them vouch (under penalty of fines and/or imprisonment) for the accuracy and completeness of their company's financial statements. This helps to ensure that investors are properly informed about the company's financial condition.

In addition, the Act imposes strict ethical rules conduct for Public Company executives in their dealings with auditors, investment bankers, analysts, and investors.

Title III- Corporate Responsibility

The Client's Audit Committee

The public company's audit committee's job is to appoint, compensate and oversee the work of any registered public accounting firm they hire. In particular, this includes resolving disagreements between

23

management and the auditor. The registered public accounting firm reports directly to the audit committee. Members of the audit committee, chosen from the Board of Directors, are independent of Management.

Independence of the Audit Committee

The Sarbanes-Oxley Act of 2002 requires that each member of the audit committee be a member of the board of directors and be independent. "Independent" means that the audit committee member cannot accept any consulting, advisory, or other compensatory fee from either the public company or the auditing firm, other than what they would normally receive in their capacity as a Member of the Board. It is thought that, because they have no vested financial interest in the results of the audit, they can be more objective in settling auditing disputes that arise between Management and the audit firm.

Complaint Procedures

The audit committee must have procedures for handling complaints about accounting, internal accounting controls, or auditing matters. It must also provide a means for employees to submit, confidentially and anonymously, their concerns regarding questionable accounting or auditing issues.

Certifications by the CEO and the CFO

The Act stipulates that the Chief Executive Officer (CEO) and the Chief Financial Officer (CFO) certify in each annual and in each quarterly report filed that they have reviewed the report, and that, to the best of their knowledge, the report "*does not contain any untrue statement of a material fact, does not omit to state a material fact necessary in order to make the statements made, and is not misleading in light of the circumstances under which such statements were made.*" (Sarbanes-Oxley Act of 2002, p. 33.)

The CEO and CFO must further certify that "*the financial statements, and other financial information included in the report, fairly present in all material respects the financial condition and results of operations of the issuer as of, and for, the periods presented in the report.*" (Sarbanes-Oxley Act of 2002, p. 33.).

In other words, they must certify that the numbers are accurate and that everything else on the report is true.

CEO and CFO Responsibility for Internal Controls

In addition, the signing officers are responsible for establishing and maintaining internal controls. They stipulate that they have designed internal controls to ensure that "*material information relating to the issuer and its consolidated subsidiaries is made known to such officers by others within those entities, particularly during the period in which the periodic reports are being prepared."* (Sarbanes-Oxley Act of 2002, p. 33.)

In other words, the signing officers attest that they have set things up to make sure they know what they ought to know.

They must further certify that they have evaluated the effectiveness of the company's internal controls within 90 days prior to the report. They must include their conclusions about the effectiveness of their internal controls in their report.

Disclosure of Deficiencies

The signing officers must disclose to the auditors and the audit committee *"...all significant deficiencies in the design or operation of internal controls which could adversely affect the issuer's ability to record, process, summarize, and report financial data."* (Sarbanes-Oxley Act of 2002, p. 33.)

In other words, if they cannot certify that all controls work effectively, they must report which controls are lacking or might not be working as well as they should.

Disclosure of All Fraud

The signing officers must also disclose any

discoveries of fraud, no matter how small, that involve management or other employees who have a significant role in the company's internal controls.

Changes in Internal Controls and Corrective Actions

The signing officers must say whether or not there were significant changes in internal controls or in other factors that could significantly affect internal controls after the date of their evaluation. They must list any corrective actions with regard to significant deficiencies and material weaknesses.

Certification of the signing officers is still required when a US public company moves its corporate head office from inside the United States to outside of the United States. For example, if a US public company moves from New York City to Paris, it is still required to meet the requirements of Sarbanes-Oxley.

Improper Influence on Conduct of Audits

The Act prohibits any officer or director of a public company from any attempt to "...*fraudulently influence, coerce, manipulate, or mislead any independent public or certified accountant engaged in the performance of an audit of the financial statements of that issuer for the purpose of rendering such financial statements materially misleading.*" (Sarbanes-Oxley Act of 2002, p. 34.)

In other words, the company cannot attempt to

influence or mislead the auditor in any way.

Forfeiture of Bonuses and Profits

The Act says that if a public company restates its financial statements due to the "...*material noncompliance of the issuer, as a result of misconduct, with any financial reporting requirement under the securities laws*" the chief executive officer and chief financial officer of the public company can be asked to reimburse the public company for any bonus or other incentive-based or equity-based compensation received. In addition, they may be asked to return any profits realized from the sale of securities within twelve months following the filing with the Securities and Exchange Commission. (Sarbanes-Oxley Act of 2002, p. 34.)

In other words, if the company ends up having to restate its financial statements, the CEO and CFO can be required to pay back their bonuses and give back any profits they made on the sale of company stock.

Blackout Periods for Directors and Executive Officers

Blackout periods are three or more consecutive business days during which specified individuals cannot trade the company's stock. Blackout periods are usually imposed prior to events that are likely to significantly affect company stock prices, such as a corporate merger or an acquisition, or when the company spins off a division. This is an attempt to eliminate the possibility of profiting through insider information.

Directors and executive officers of a public company that receive stock as compensation cannot trade their company's stock during any blackout period. Blackout periods for Directors and Executive officers are usually much longer than the blackout periods imposed on other employees or employee group retirement plans, sometimes up to six months.

Any profit realized by a director or executive officer from trades during the blackout period is recoverable regardless of the intention of the director or executive officer. Legal action to recover profits from the transaction can be initiated by the company or by any shareholder on behalf of the company within two years.

30 Days Notice

The public company has an obligation to notify in a timely fashion the director or officer and the Securities and Exchange Commission of any blackout period. This means that, before the beginning of any blackout period, the plan administrator of an individual account plan must notify the plan participants and beneficiaries who are affected.

The plan administrator must provide, in writing (or electronically if appropriate), at least 30 days in advance of the blackout period:

- The reasons for the blackout period
- Identification of the investments affected
- The expected beginning date
- The length of the blackout period

The Secretary of Labor establishes the criteria used by the public company plan administrator to decide who is affected by the blackout period, in addition to the timing and length of the blackout period. The administrator must notify everyone who is affected by the blackout so that they will not buy or sell stock during the blackout period. If these participants do buy or sell stock during the blackout period, they will have to pay back any profits from those transactions.

If a plan administrator fails to give the appropriate notice, the administrator can be fined $100 per day for each violation. Every single participant or beneficiary is treated as a separate violation.

Professional Responsibility for Attorneys

The Sarbanes-Oxley Act of 2002 requires an attorney who represents a public company before the Securities and Exchange Commission to report any violations of securities law or breach of fiduciary duty by the company to the chief legal counsel or the chief executive officer of the company, and subsequently to the audit committee and to the Board of Directors if there is no appropriate response.

TITLE IV - Enhanced Financial Disclosures

Required Disclosures

Accuracy

This section of the Sarbanes-Oxley Act of 2002 specifies that public accounting firms identify any correcting adjustments included in the financial statements. These adjustments must be follow generally accepted accounting principles (GAAP) and the rules and regulations of the Securities and Exchange Commission.

Off-Balance Sheet Transactions

The Act stipulates that all material off-balance sheet transactions, arrangements, and obligations (including contingent obligations) with companies that affect the following should be included in the audit report:

- Financial condition of the company
- Results of operations
- Liquidity
- Capital expenditures
- Capital resources
- Revenues
- Expenses

Pro Forma Financial Information

Pro forma financial information (information based on assumptions) included in any report filed with the Securities and Exchange Commission (or that is part of a public disclosure or press release), must follow generally accepted accounting principles (GAAP) and cannot be presented in a misleading manner. In the past, many companies presented Pro Forma statements using overly optimistic revenue projections to induce increases in the share price and corresponding increases in executive bonuses and/or the value of their share options.

Executive Loans

Section 402 of the Act prohibits a public company from extending, arranging or maintaining credit in the form of a personal loan to any director or executive officer of that public company. This provision is intended to prevent companies from using these loans as forms of executive compensation, which might be difficult for the average investor to detect. These loans, often substantial, often facilitated the exercising of stock options by executives who stood to profit the most from inflated stock prices. For example, Dennis Kozlowski, the former CEO of Tyco owed $61 million, while Bernie Ebbers, the former WorldCom CEO, owed $400 million to their respective companies.

However, the Act specifically excludes a home

improvement loan, or other credit that is provided in the ordinary course of the consumer credit business of a public company which is made on the same terms as that offered to the general public.

Disclosure of Transactions Involving Management

Who must disclose?

The Sarbanes-Oxley Act of 2002 requires disclosure from every person who:

- Owns more than 10% of any class of any stock
- Is a director or an officer

To whom must they disclose?

They must disclose to the Securities and Exchange Commission and the stock exchange (if the stock is traded on a national stock exchange).

When must they disclose?

The disclosure is required:

- At the time of the registration of the stock on a national securities exchange
- Within 10 days after he or she becomes more than 10% shareholder
- Within 10 days after he or she becomes director

- Within 10 days after he or she becomes officer
- At the time of the purchase of stock using a security-based swap agreement
- At the time of the sale of stock using a security-based swap agreement

What must they disclose?

A greater than 10% shareholder, director, or officer needs to file a statement declaring:

- The amount of all company stock owned at the date of filing
- Any changes in ownership since the most recent filing
- Any purchases of the security-based swap agreements since the most recent filing
- Any sales of the security-based swap agreements since the most recent filing

How must they disclose?

The disclosure statement must be filed electronically. The Securities and Exchange Commission makes the statements available on a publicly accessible Internet site by the end of the following business day. The public company must also provide that statement on their corporate website the following business day.

Management Assessment of Internal Controls

The registered public accounting firm that prepares the audit of a public company must attest and report independently on the assessment of the company's internal controls made by the management as part of its audit engagement.

Code of Ethics Required for Senior Financial Officers

The Sarbanes-Oxley Act of 2002 talks about the establishment of code of ethics for senior financial officers of public companies. Public companies must disclose to the Securities and Exchange Commission whether they have adopted a code of ethics for senior financial officers. The Act specifies that these codes of conduct also apply to the Chief Financial Officer (CFO) and the comptroller.

The code of ethics should cover the handling of actual or apparent conflicts of interest between personal and professional relationships through, "...*full, fair, accurate, timely, and understandable disclosure...*", and compliance with applicable governmental rules and regulations. (Sarbanes-Oxley Act of 2002, p. 46.) This says that the company's code of ethics for its senior financial officers must be easy to understand, and clear about the required disclosures. Any changes in the code of ethics adopted by the company must also be reported to the Securities and Exchange Commission.

Disclosure of Audit Committee Financial Expert

The Sarbanes-Oxley Act of 2002 requires that the audit committee appointed by a public company's board of directors must be comprised of at least one "financial expert". This "financial expert" should have an understanding of generally accepted accounting principles (GAAP) and financial statements.

The "financial expert" should:

- Have experience in the preparation or auditing of financial statements of similar companies
- Know how to prepare estimates, accruals, and reserves
- Have experience with internal accounting controls
- Understand how the audit committee functions

Enhanced Review of Periodic Disclosures

The Securities and Exchange Commission has a duty to review the disclosures made by public companies whose stock is listed on a national securities exchange on a regular basis.

The criteria the SEC uses to schedule reviews earlier than the minimum 3-year period include:

- Material restatements of financial results
- Significant volatility in stock price

- Large market capitalization
- Disparities in price to earning ratios
- Operations that significantly affect any material sector of the economy

Disclosures Need to be Current and Understandable

Public companies are required to immediately disclose in plain English to the public any additional information concerning material changes in the financial condition or operations. For example, if a company's revenue is adversely affected by a court decision, immediate disclosure to the public and to the Securities and Exchange Commission is required

TITLE X - Corporate Tax Returns

This title, with only one sentence in it, requires that the chief executive officer sign the corporation's Federal income tax return.

Chapter 3 Summary

• The Act makes Public Company executives personally accountable for the accuracy and completeness of their company's financial statements.

• A public company audit committee member cannot accept any consulting, advisory, or other compensatory fee from either the public company or the auditing firm, other than what they would normally receive in their capacity as a Member of the Board.

• Certification of the signing officers is still required even if a US public company moves its corporate head office outside of the United States.

• If a company ends up having to restate its financial statements, the CEO and CFO can be required to pay back their bonuses and give back any profits they made on the sale of company stock.

• Directors and executive officers of a public company cannot trade their company's stock during a blackout period. Any profit from trades during the blackout period is recoverable regardless of the intention of the director or executive officer.

• All material off-balance sheet transactions, arrangements, and obligations (including contingent obligations) that have a material effect on the financial condition of the company must be included in the audit report.

• Pro forma financial information must follow generally accepted accounting principles (GAAP) and cannot be presented in a misleading manner.

•Section 402 of the Act prohibits a public company from extending, arranging or maintaining credit in the form of a personal loan to any director or executive officer of the company. This provision is intended to prevent companies from using these loans as forms of executive compensation, which might be difficult for the average investor to detect.

The Events That Preceded Enron   4

The Sarbanes-Oxley Act of 2002 ordered five major studies to provide in-depth analysis of the events that preceded Enron. What is interesting about these findings is that blame seems to be equally shared among public company executives, auditors, analysts, and investment bankers. Any one of them could have blown the whistle, but none did.

TITLE VII - Studies and Reports

Section 701
GAO Study of Public Accounting Firms

The Sarbanes-Oxley Act of 2002 required that the GAO (General Accounting Office) conduct a comprehensive study with three main objectives:

- To determine the factors leading to the consolidation of public accounting firms
- To examine the problems faced by business organizations that has resulted from limited

competition among public accounting firms
- To ascertain whether Federal or State regulations impeded competition among public accounting firms

General Accounting Office Findings

The Audit Market is an Oligopoly

This study was completed in July 2003. According to the General Accounting Office, the audit market for large public companies is an oligopoly, with the largest firms auditing the vast majority of public companies and smaller firms facing significant barriers to entry into the market.

Mergers among the largest firms in the 1980s and 1990s and the dissolution of Arthur Andersen in 2002 significantly increased concentration among the largest firms, known as the "Big 4", namely:

- Deloitte & Touche
- Ernst & Young
- PricewaterhouseCoopers
- KPMG

These four firms currently audit over 78 percent of all U.S. public companies. The Sarbanes-Oxley Act of 2002 has had a very significant impact on these four major auditing firms who are being watched very closely. The upside for them is that their revenues are up because of the increased demand by public company clients who are rushing to meet compliance deadlines.

Unfortunately, for smaller firms, this has had the unwanted effect of making competition with the "Big 4" even more difficult in the public company auditing arena. However, the Sarbanes-Oxley Act has opened up consulting opportunities for smaller firms to help public companies become Sarbanes-Oxley compliant. These consulting opportunities are not available to "Big 4" firms because they cannot accept consulting contracts from public companies when they are engaged as their auditor.

Pessimistic Outlook for Increased Competition

The GAO said that market forces were not likely to result in the expansion of the Big 4. In fact, they said they could actually see a further reduction in the number of major accounting firms. The GAO found that smaller accounting firms faced significant barriers to entry into the large public company audit market. The GAO believes that consolidation made it more difficult for some smaller companies to raise capital for start up or expansion. Concentration of the audit market raised concerns in the areas of potential choice, price, quality, and concentration risk.

Continuing Increases in Fees

The GAO found that fees increased, and

commented that the trend was expected to continue as the audit environment responded to ongoing changes in the audit market.

Section 702
SEC Study of Credit Rating Agencies

The Sarbanes-Oxley Act of 2002 ordered the Securities and Exchange Commission to look at the role and function of credit rating agencies in the operation of the securities market. What everyone wanted to know was how the credit rating agencies could have rated Enron Corporation as a good credit risk until just four days before the company declared bankruptcy.

Conclusions

The Report concluded that, in the case of Enron, the credit rating agencies *"...displayed a disappointing lack of diligence in their coverage and assessment of that company..."* (SEC Report on the Role and Function of Credit Rating Agencies in the Operations of Securities Markets, p. 6.)

Simply put, the study questioned the credibility of credit rating agencies.

The SEC reported that, in recent years, the importance of credit ratings to investors had increased significantly, influencing a public company's access to, and cost of, capital. Credit ratings affect securities markets in many ways, including a public company's access to capital and the structure of financial transactions, as well as its cost of capital.

NRSRO's

Nationally recognized statistical rating organizations, or NRSROs, include Moody's Investors Service, Inc. ("Moody's"), Fitch, Inc. ("Fitch"), and the Standard and Poor's Division of the McGraw-Hill Companies Inc. ("S&P"). The requirement that the credit rating agency be nationally recognized was designed to ensure that its ratings were reliable, but it did not appear to be working.

Monitoring by Credit Rating Agencies

Rating agencies monitor credit ratings by reviewing corporate filings, watching industry trends, and through discussion with corporate management.

Rating agency representatives told the Securities and Exchange Commission that they do not conduct formal audits of rated companies or search for fraud, and that the nature of their analysis is largely dependent on the quality of information provided to them. In other words, they trusted the companies and did not verify any of the information for themselves.

According to the SEC, examination of the NRSROs revealed several concerns. These included obvious potential conflicts of interest because public companies paid the NRSROs for their ratings. Another area was the marketing by the NRSROs of other services to public companies, such as pre-rating assessments and corporate consulting, and a corresponding dependence by the NRSROs on revenue from public companies.

Witnesses said that they were concerned that informal verbal contacts between subscribers (the companies which are the rating agency clients) and rating agency analysts increased the risk of improper disclosure of confidential information provided by the issuers to subscribers by analysts. It was feared that these disclosures were a means of offering analysts the opportunity to profit from insider information in return for a favorable rating. Other witnesses stated that analysts could inappropriately warn subscribers about upcoming ratings changes and their market impact.

Not surprisingly, the Securities and Exchange Commission study concluded that one of the most significant barriers into the credit rating business is the current dominance of a few, well-capitalized rating agencies.

Section 703
SEC Study of Violations by Securities Professionals

The Sarbanes-Oxley Act of 2002 ordered the Securities and Exchange Commission to examine, based on information for the period from January 1, 1998, to December 31, 2001, the instances of securities professionals who violated Federal securities laws.

Results

The study revealed that, during the four-year period, (calendar years 1998, 1999, 2000 and 2001), 1596 securities professionals were found to have aided and abetted violations of and/or violated the Federal securities laws in actions brought by the securities and Exchange Commission. (SEC Study and Report on Violations by Securities Professionals, p. 1.)

An additional 117 securities professionals, while not violating the Federal securities laws, were included in the study because they either failed to reasonably supervise employees or engaged in improper professional conduct.

The securities professionals most frequently found to have violated the Federal securities laws were individuals associated with broker-dealers:

- Registered representatives or branch managers (788)
- Broker-dealer firms (236)
- Individuals associated with investment advisers (172)

The most common types of cases against these securities professionals involved:

- Securities offerings (385)
- Fraud against broker-dealer customers (323)
- Investment adviser violations (228)

Sanctions and penalties

The most frequently ordered sanctions were:

- Permanent injunctions (782)
(They can no longer work in their field)
- Civil monetary penalties (730) (fines)
- Bars from association with broker-dealers (434)
- Disgorgement (673) (recovery of illegal profits)
- Permanent cease-and-desist orders (613)

An example of a permanent cease-and-desist order is the August 13, 2003 decision where the SEC ordered former Tyco auditor Richard P. Scalzo, CPA, to "cease and desist violating antifraud provisions" and was barred from practicing as an accountant.

Disgorgement is a civil enforcement remedy that enables the Securities and Exchange Commission to recover profits from violators of Federal securities laws, even years after the violations occurred. Disgorgement in the amount of $799,355,572 was assessed against 555 securities professionals. At first glance this seems like a lot of money, however, if you do the math, this is an average of $144,000 penalty per person…not that much considering the profits some of them must have made.

Section 704
SEC Study of Violations of Reporting Requirements

The Securities and Exchange Commission was ordered by the Sarbanes-Oxley Act of 2002 to review and analyze all enforcement actions by the Securities and Exchange Commission involving violations of reporting requirements and restatements of financial statements, over the 5-year period preceding the Sarbanes-Oxley Act of 2002. The purpose of the study was to identify areas of reporting that are most susceptible to fraud.

Results

The Study revealed that the majority of the persons held responsible for the accounting violations were members of public company senior management. The Study found that 157 of the 227 enforcement matters involved charges against at least one senior manager.

Charges were brought against:

- 75 Chairmen of the Board
- 111 Chief Executive Officers ("CEOs")
- 111 Presidents
- 105 Chief Financial Officers ("CFOs")
- 21 Chief Operating Officers ("COOs")
- 16 Chief Accounting Officers ("CAOs")
- 27 Vice Presidents ("VPs") of Finance
- 18 auditing firms

- 89 individual auditors

The Study identified several areas of reporting *"susceptible to fraud and other improper conduct"*:

- Improper revenue recognition (126)
- Improper expense recognition (101)
- Improper accounting in connection with business combinations (23)
- Inadequate disclosures in Management Discussion and Analysis ("MD&A") and elsewhere in public company filings (43)
- Failure to disclose related party transactions (23)
- Inappropriate accounting for non-monetary transactions (19)
- Improper accounting for foreign payments in violation of the Foreign Corrupt Practices Act ("FCPA") (6)
- Improper use of off-balance sheet arrangements (3)
- Improper use of non-GAAP financial measures (2)

The Study found that revenue recognition was an area that is highly susceptible to financial reporting violations. Of the 227 enforcement matters during the Study period, 126 involved some form of improper revenue recognition. The majority of these enforcement matters involved improper timing (81 of 126 enforcement matters) and fictitious revenue (80 of 126 enforcement matters). These violations included falsification of documents, such as sales invoices. At least one representative of senior management was charged in

104 of the 126 enforcement matters.

The Study also found that 57 enforcement matters resulted in charges for auditing violations, often as a result of:

- Auditors accepting management representations without verification
- Auditors not following proper analytical and substantive procedures
- Auditors failing to gain sufficient evidence regarding representations in issuer financial statements

Section 705
GAO Study of Investment Banks

The Sarbanes-Oxley Act of 2002 called for the General Accounting Office to conduct a study on whether investment banks and financial advisers assisted issuers in manipulating their earnings and hiding their true financial condition.

Investment Banks and Enron

The Sarbanes-Oxley Act of 2002 directed the General Accounting Office to look specifically at the role of investment banks and financial advisors in the collapse of the Enron Corporation. They were directed to review the design and implementation of derivatives transactions, transactions involving special purpose vehicles, and other financial arrangements that may have had the effect of altering the company's reported financial statements in ways that masked the true financial picture of the company.

Investment Banks and Global Crossing

With regard to Global Crossing, they were asked to look into transactions involving swaps of fiber optic cable capacity that may have had the effect of altering the company's reported financial statements in ways that clouded the true financial picture of the company, and transactions intended to manipulate revenue streams, obtain loans, and move liabilities off balance sheets without changing the economic and business risks faced by the companies to hide a company's financial picture.

Investment Banks and SPE's

Investment banks offer not only traditional services such as securities underwriting, but also provide advice on and assistance in creating different types of structured finance transactions, such as SPE's. An SPE is a legal entity created by another entity (a sponsor) to carry out a specified purpose or activity. An SPE is often a financing vehicle that allows a sponsor entity to transfer assets to the SPE in exchange for cash, including "prepay transactions", which are transactions that involve a contract for a service or product to be delivered at a later date.

Results

The General Accounting Office study concluded that certain investment banks facilitated and participated in complex financial transactions with Enron despite allegedly knowing that the intent of the transactions was to manipulate and obscure Enron's true financial condition. However, the investment banks involved in the transactions contended that their actions were appropriate and that Enron had not revealed its true purpose in obtaining their assistance.

The GAO concluded that while investment banks are not responsible for the financial reporting of their clients, if it is proven that the investment banks knowingly assisted Enron in engaging in securities law violations, the Securities and Exchange Commission has the authority to take legal action against them. It is a violation of law for investment banks to facilitate transactions that they know will materially misstate the client's financial statements.

Investment Banks and Research Analysts

The study found that investment bankers of certain securities firms allegedly pressured their research analysts covering Enron and Global Crossing to issue favorable or misleading investment recommendations (i.e., buy ratings) in order to keep or obtain lucrative investment banking work from the companies.

The study concluded that the adequacy and effectiveness of barriers between the research and investment banking functions of securities firms that offer both services were not sufficient.

Chapter 4 Summary

• The audit market for large public companies is an oligopoly, with the largest firms auditing the vast majority of public companies and smaller firms facing significant barriers to entry into the market. The "Big 4" firms, Deloitte & Touche, Ernst & Young, Pricewaterhouse Coopers, and KPMG currently audit over 78 percent of all U.S. public companies

• Consulting opportunities have arisen for smaller firms to help public companies become Sarbanes-Oxley compliant. These consulting opportunities are not available to "Big 4" firms because they cannot accept consulting contracts from public companies when they are engaged as their auditor.

• Nationally recognized statistical rating organizations, or NRSROs, do not conduct formal audits of rated companies or search for fraud, and the nature of their analysis is largely dependent on the quality of information provided to them. In other words, they trust the companies and do not verify any of the information for themselves. There are also obvious potential conflicts of interest because public companies paid the NRSROs for their ratings.

• Studies found that revenue recognition was an area that is highly susceptible to financial reporting violations. Of the 227 enforcement matters during the Study period, 126 involved some form of improper revenue recognition. The majority of these enforcement matters involved improper timing (81 of 126 enforcement matters) and fictitious revenue (80 of 126 enforcement matters). These violations included falsification of documents, such as sales invoices.

• Studies found that investment bankers of certain securities firms allegedly pressured their research analysts covering Enron and Global Crossing to issue favorable or misleading investment recommendations (i.e., buy ratings) in order to keep or obtain lucrative investment banking work from the companies.

Enhancing Investor Confidence

The Sarbanes-Oxley Act of 2002 gets serious when it comes to handing out fines and prison terms. Fines can be as high as $5 million dollars and those who get caught can end up spending many years in jail. That's why Worldcom and Enron's executives are spending lots of money on lawyers.

TITLE VIII
Corporate and Criminal Fraud Accountability

The Act imposes severe penalties for the destruction, alteration, or falsification of records in Federal investigations and bankruptcy. This provision is intended to be a deterrent for anyone thinking of duplicating the actions of the Andersen auditors who destroyed Enron records.

"Whoever knowingly alters, destroys, mutilates, concealts, covers up, falsifies, or makes a false entry in any record, document, or tangible object with the intent to impede, obstruct, or influence the investigation or proper

administration of any matter within the jurisdiction of any department or agency of the United States or any case filed under title 11, or in relation to or contemplation of any such matter or case, shall be fined under this title, imprisoned not more than 20 years, or both." (Sarbanes Oxley Act of 2002, p. 56.)

Destruction of Corporate Audit Records

Accountants must keep audit records for 5 years

Section 802 (Subsection 1520) says that any accountant who conducts an audit must maintain all audit or review work papers for 5 years from the end of the fiscal period in which the audit or review was concluded. Violators can be fined and imprisoned up to 10 years.

Section 103 specifies that the audit firm must keep the audit records for at least 7 years.

Debts Non-Dischargeable

The Sarbanes-Oxley Act of 2002 specifies that violation of securities fraud laws is grounds for not discharging debts that would otherwise be discharged, such as bankruptcy debts.

Statute of Limitations for Securities Fraud

The Act sets the statute of limitations for securities

fraud 5 years after the violation occurred or 2 years after the discovery of the facts. This applies only to proceedings started after July 30, 2002. Prior to the Sarbanes-Oxley Act of 2002, the limit was 3 years after the violation occurred or 1 year after discovery of the facts (Section 10 (b) of the Exchange Act).

The Whistleblower Clause

There is a whistleblower clause (Section 806) that says no officer, employee, contractor, subcontractor, or agent may discriminate against a public company employee who provides information or assists in an investigation of a violation of any regulation of the Securities and Exchange Commission, or any provision of Federal law relating to fraud against shareholders. Section 806 says that employees of public companies have 90 days to file a complaint with the Secretary of Labor if they feel they have been harassed or been victims of discrimination because they have reported their employer's violations to the Securities and Exchange Commission. If the whistleblower proves their case, their employer can be ordered to give them their job back, compensatory damages, legal fees and expert witness fees.

Section 1107 of the Sarbanes-Oxley Act of 2002 prohibits any retaliation against informants, whether or not they are employees of public companies:

"Whoever knowingly, with the intent to retaliate,

takes any action harmful to any person, including interference with the lawful employment or livelihood of any person, for providing to a law enforcement officer any truthful information relating to the commission or possible commission of any Federal offense, shall be fined under this title or imprisoned not more than 10 years, or both."
(Sarbanes-Oxley Act of 2002, p.66.)

Criminal Penalties for Defrauding Shareholders

The Sarbanes-Oxley Act of 2002 imposes stiff criminal penalties for defrauding shareholders of publicly traded companies. There are penalties for anyone who knowingly sets out to obtain, by fraudulent means, any money or property in connection with the purchase of stock. In other words, anyone who makes false representations, such as a broker or dealer, about the company in order to induce someone to buy the company's stock, can be fined and/or imprisoned up to 25 years. This provision is meant to prevent brokers from making false or exaggerated claims to induce investors to buy public company stock.

TITLE IX - White-collar Crime Penalty Enhancements

Attempt and Conspiracy

The Sarbanes-Oxley Act of 2002 says that trying to commit an offence is the same as actually committing the offence.

"Any person who attempts or conspires to commit any offense under this chapter shall be subject to the same penalties as those prescribed for the offense, the commission of which was the object of the attempt or conspiracy." (Sarbanes-Oxley Act of 2002, p.61.)

Criminal Penalties for Mail and Wire Fraud

Mail and wire fraud are Federal crimes that make it an offence for anyone to use the mail or to use interstate wire communications facilities in carrying out a scheme to defraud. The Sarbanes-Oxley Act of 2002 says that each separate use of the mail or interstate wire facilities in furtherance of a scheme to defraud constitutes a separate offence. The Act stipulates that anyone convicted of mail or wire fraud can be imprisoned up to 20 years.

The Employee Retirement Income Security Act of 1974 (ERISA-Section 501)

A person who embezzles or steals funds, securities, property, or other assets of a labor organization of which he or she is an officer, or by which he is employed, can be fined up to $100,000 and imprisoned for up to 10 years.

Failure of Corporate Officers to Certify Financial Reports

Corporate officers (the chief executive officer and the chief financial officer) who certify any statement that does not comply with all the requirements of the Sarbanes-Oxley Act of 2002 can be fined up to $1,000,000 and imprisoned up to 10 years.

Corporate officers (the chief executive officer and the chief financial officer) who willfully certify any statement knowing that the periodic report accompanying the statement does not comply with all the requirements of the Sarbanes-Oxley Act of 2002 can be fined up to $5,000,000 and imprisoned up to 20 years.

CFO.com reported on November 19, 2004, *"According to Netherlands-based research firm A.R.C. Morgan, at companies that disclosure a material weakness, nearly 62 percent of chief financial officers either leave the company or are pushed out immediately before the announcement or within three months afterward."*

More and more qualified people are reluctant to take on the role of CEO or CFO of public companies because of the personal liability involved. Many others are rethinking Board membership offers because they risk putting their reputation on the line. As well, insurance to cover Board members is getting more expensive and more difficult to obtain.

TITLE XI - Corporate Fraud Accountability

Tampering with a Record or Impeding an Official Proceeding

"Whoever corruptly- (1) alters, destroys, mutilates, or conceals a record, document, or other object, or attempts to do so, with the intent to impair the object's integrity or availability for use in an official proceeding; or (2) otherwise obstructs, influences, or impedes any official proceeding, or attempts to do so, shall be fined under this title or imprisoned not more than 20 years, or both." (Sarbanes-Oxley Act of 2002, p.63.)

Temporary Freeze Authority

If the Securities and Exchange Commission suspects a public company to be in violation of any Federal securities law, it can freeze any payments to any of its directors, officers, partners, controlling persons, agents, and employees up to 45 days.

If the Securities and Exchange Commission does not bring a charge against any of the parties, then the money is released back to the public company at the end of the period of the temporary order.

Persons Barred From Serving as Officers or Directors

The Securities and Exchange Commission can issue a permanent or temporary order to prohibit, conditionally or unconditionally, anyone who has violated the Sarbanes-Oxley Act of 2002 from acting as an officer or director of any public company if the conduct of that person demonstrates that they are not fit to serve as an officer or director of any issuer. Anyone convicted of contravening this order can be fined up to $5,000,000, or imprisoned not more than 20 years, or both. Public companies can be fined up to $25,000,000.

Chapter 5 Summary

• In response to the actions of the Andersen auditors who destroyed Enron records, the Act imposes severe penalties for the destruction, alteration, or falsification of records in Federal investigations and bankruptcy.

• Auditors must keep audit records for 5 years, audit firms for 7 years.

• Debts are nondischargeable if they were incurred in violation of securities fraud laws.

• The Act changes the statute of limitations for securities fraud to 5 years after the violation occurred or 2 years after the discovery of the facts.

• There is a whistleblower clause (Section 806) that says no officer, employee, contractor, subcontractor, or agent may discriminate against a public company employee who provides information or assists in an investigation of a violation of any regulation of the Securities and Exchange Commission, or any provision of Federal law relating to fraud against shareholders

• The Act says that trying to commit an offence is the same as actually committing the offence.

• Corporate officers who certify any statement that does not comply with all the requirements of the Act can be fined up to $1,000,000 and imprisoned up to 10 years.

• A person who embezzles or steals funds, securities, property, or other assets of a labor organization of which he or she is an officer, or by which he is employed, can be fined up to $100,000 and imprisoned for up to 10 years.

Conflict of Interest

6

The Sarbanes-Oxley Act of 2002 addresses the issue of the independence of auditors, analysts, and investment bankers.

Before Enron, investors counted on auditors, and to a lesser extent, analysts, and investment bankers, to protect their interests by ringing the alarm if something was not quite right. Unfortunately, these players stood to make large sums of money if they did not alert investors. Enron, its executives, auditors, analysts, and investment bankers got away with it for a while only because they participated in a conspiracy of silence that sacrificed objectivity for money, and careers for short-term gain. This collusion and lack of objectivity was a major contributing factor to the events that led to Enron's collapse and the enactment of the Sarbanes Oxley Act of 2002.

TITLE II - Auditor Independence

Services Outside the Scope of Practice of Auditors

In an effort to prevent the type of conflicts of interest that ultimately resulted in the collapse of Enron, the Act prohibits auditors from providing additional paid services to their auditing clients.

Registered public accounting firms that provide audit services cannot, at the same time, provide non-audit services such as:

- Bookkeeping
- Information systems design and implementation
- Appraisal or valuation services
- Fairness opinions
- Actuarial services
- Internal audit outsourcing services
- Management and human resources functions
- Broker or investment banking services
- Legal services
- Expert services unrelated to the audit

The public company's audit committee must pre-approve other non-audit services not on this list, such as tax services. However, the pre-approval requirement is not needed for non-audit services that are not more than 5% of the total amount of annual revenues paid by the client to its auditor if they are:

- Promptly brought to the attention of the audit committee
- Approved prior to the completion of the audit
- Disclosed to investors

Audit Partner Rotation

A registered public accounting firm is not permitted to provide audit services to a public company if the audit lead, or the audit partner responsible for reviewing the audit, has performed audit services for that public company in each of the 5 previous fiscal years.

This rotation is intended to reduce the risk of personal relationships interfering with the auditor's independence and objectivity.

Auditor Reports to Audit Committee

The registered public accounting firm that performs an audit is required to tell the audit committee of the public company:

- All critical accounting policies and practices to be used
- All alternative treatments of financial information within generally accepted accounting principles that have been discussed with management officials and the consequences of using them
- What treatment the firm recommends
- All important written communications between

the firm and management of the issuer (such as any management letter or schedule of unadjusted differences)

Conflicts of Interest

The Sarbanes-Oxley Act of 2002 does not permit a registered public accounting firm to perform any audit service for a public company if the firm employed any of the following within a year prior to the start of the audit:

- Chief Executive Officer
- Chief Financial Officer
- Controller
- Chief Accounting Officer

Non-Registered Public Accounting Firms

The Act says the standards applied by the Public Company Accounting Oversight Board do not generally apply to small and medium sized non-registered public accounting firms. The Public Company Accounting Oversight Board and other regulatory authorities can decide which standards applicable given the size and nature of the business of the accounting firms and the clients of those firms.

However, small and medium sized non-registered public accounting firm are protecting their reputations by using the same standards as much as possible.

TITLE V - Analyst Conflicts of Interest

Treatment of Securities Analysts by Registered Securities Associations and National Securities Exchanges

Purpose

The Act sets out rules regarding possible conflicts of interest when securities analysts recommend equity securities in research reports and public appearances. The objectives of these regulations are to:

- Improve the objectivity of research
- Provide investors with more useful and reliable information

Investment Bankers Must Wait for Publication of the Research Report

In an attempt to make securities analysts more objective and independent, the Sarbanes-Oxley Act of 2002 limits the prepublication approval of research reports by employees of the broker or dealer who are involved in investment banking activities, or people not directly responsible for investment research, other than legal or compliance staff.

In other words, investment bankers have to wait until the report has been made public, like all other investors.

Rules Against Retaliation For An Unfavorable Report

These rules are meant to restrict the supervision and compensatory evaluation of securities analysts to officials employed by the broker or dealer who are not engaged in investment banking activities. In other words, the analysts cannot report to anyone in the investment banking side of their companies. The rules also prohibit a broker or dealer and their employees who are involved with investment banking activities from retaliating or threatening to retaliate against any securities analyst because of an unfavorable research report.

In other words, the securities analysts who are involved in investment banking activities and the public companies who are the subject of research reports are prohibited from influencing the results of those research reports.

Time Limitations ("Quiet" periods)

A broker or dealer who participates, or is going to participate, in a public offering of securities of a public company as underwriters or dealers cannot publish or distribute research reports relating to that public company within 40 days following an initial public offering or 10 days after secondary offerings.

Disclosure of Conflicts of Interest by Securities Analysts

A securities analyst is someone who is responsible for the preparation of a research report. This also includes anyone who reports directly or indirectly to a securities analyst.

Research Report

A research report includes an analysis of equity securities of individual companies or industries used to make an investment decision.

Disclosure Rules for Public Appearances and Research Reports

Securities analysts must disclose, in public appearances and in each research report, any conflicts of interest that should have been known by the securities analyst to exist at the time of the appearance or the date of distribution of the report.

These conflicts include:

• Investments in the company
• Compensation received by the securities analyst from the company
• Whether the company is or has been a client in the last year
• Types of services provided
• Any investment banking revenues received

Far-reaching Powers of Enforcement

The Securities and Exchange Commission enforces the securities laws by monitoring and regulating the accounting profession. As well as setting standards for auditing and accounting practices, the Securities and Exchange Commission can start legal, administrative, or disciplinary action against any registered public accounting firm at any time. These can range from censure to disbarment, and include fines of up to $1 million, and prison terms of up to 20 years.

Chapter 6 Summary

• Enron, its executives, auditors, analysts, and investment bankers participated in a conspiracy of silence that sacrificed objectivity for money, and careers for short-term gain. This collusion and lack of objectivity was a major contributing factor to the events that led to Enron's collapse and the enactment of the Sarbanes Oxley Act of 2002.

• In an effort to prevent the type of conflicts of interest that ultimately resulted in the collapse of Enron, the Sarbanes-Oxley Act of 2002 prohibits auditors from providing additional paid services to their auditing clients.

• A registered public accounting firm is not permitted to provide audit services to a public company if the audit lead, or the audit partner responsible for reviewing the audit, has performed audit services for that public company in each of the 5 previous fiscal years.

• Securities analysts who are involved in investment banking activities and the public companies who are the subject of research reports are prohibited from influencing the results of those research reports.

The Compliance Process   7

Financial Controls:
The Backbone of Risk Management Plans

The Sarbanes-Oxley Act of 2002 makes CEO's and CFO's personally responsible for producing financial statements that accurately portray the financial state of the company. It asks them to make sure that the reports are complete and that nothing is left out. However, the Act does not specify exactly how they are supposed to make sure that all material facts are disclosed. They leave it to company executives to put controls in place to make sure they know everything they ought to know. This is the aspect of the Act that frightens most executives.

Section 404 of the Act requires companies to document the internal controls that their company uses to ensure the accuracy of their financial reports. It requires companies to identify key business processes, the controls overriding the processes, and any vulnerability in these controls. Many companies have found it necessary to restate their year-end financial statements as a result of their findings after performing these Section 404 assessments.

Starting At the Top

Financial controls start at the top and must trickle down. The Board has a mandate from shareholders to provide the best possible return on their investment. The Board sets broad, strategic goals for the company but should leave the day-to-day running the company to the CEO and Senior Management. Senior Management in turn delegates to Middle Management for executing the operational plans by Department or Function.

The CEO sees the big picture, while each step down sees progressively smaller and smaller pieces of the puzzle. The people at the top, who are the only ones who see the whole picture, are personally responsible, but the people at the bottom are the ones who actually do the work.

The Process

The process of meeting the requirement of Section 404 consists of several steps, first from an overall company position, then from a departmental or functional perspective.

A Simple Model

Here is how one company might work through

the Section 404 compliance process. This simple model illustrates a methodology that is easy to follow. In practice, it is easily expanded to encompass the most complicated corporate structures.

The Steps

1) Establishment of overall company goals through the Board of Directors

The first step of the process is to articulate the company's overall key objectives. The shareholders, through the company's Board of Directors, determine the long-term goals they want their company to achieve. The Board must govern rather than manage. It sets broad objectives, but leaves the method of reaching that goal to the CEO and Senior Management. For example, if the Board says it wants a return on investment of 5%, it will leave the formulation and execution of a plan to get a ROI of 5%. The Board's job is to first clearly define the shareholders', and by extension, the company's expectations.

2) Board directives to Senior Management for achieving company goals

Once the Board has determined the goals of the company, it directs Senior Management by defining the limits of Senior Management's authority, the criteria by which Senior Management's success will be measured, and providing the resources necessary for the achievement of those goals, and a feedback mechanism. At this level, the goals are long-range ones (strategic).

The Board should communicate the framework within which it expects the CEO and Senior Management to accomplish the company's objectives. The Board should adopt a philosophy of giving Senior Management guidance but not limiting them in how they act. The only limitations imposed on Senior Management by the Board should be to specify what methods of achieving the company's objectives are not acceptable. For example, Senior Management may be free to choose whatever product development strategy will produce the desired results, but, the Board may specify that any method chosen must not involve the inhumane treatment of animals, or it could specify that it cannot harm the environment, because of restrictions based on the expressed wishes of the shareholders.

3) Senior Management gives directives to Department or Function Managers for achieving company and Department or Function goals

Having received its directives from the Board of Directors, Senior Management develops a plan to get things done. This overall plan in turn becomes a series of smaller plans that encompasses medium to short-term operational goals. Each of these plans is entrusted to a Department or Function Manager who will be responsible for executing the operational plan assigned to them.

Senior Management has many options to choose from in developing its plan, but will typically provide a more focused, limited plan for each individual Department/Function Manager. The level of discretion decreases as the directives go down the chain of command.

For example, Senior Management may decide to cut overall costs by 10% and will choose how much each Department or Function will contribute to the cost-cutting measure. It may ask sales to reduce costs by 12%, but require that IT cut costs only by 8%. In turn, each Department or Function Manager will have to decide how to achieve these cut backs within their own Department or Function. Although there is some amount of flexibility in choosing which costs to cut at the Department or Function level, it is not nearly as much discretion as that given to Senior Management by the Board.

The Company Process

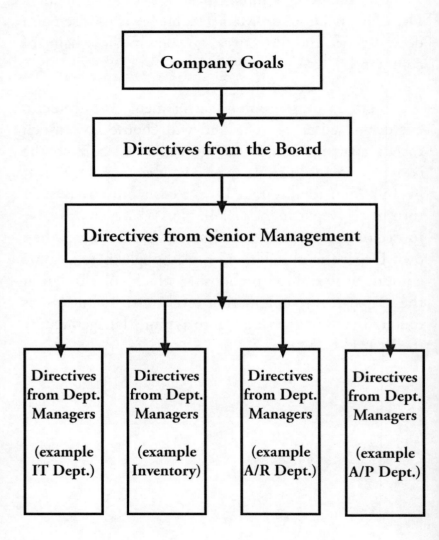

Department or Function Steps

1) Department or Function directives to staff for achieving goals

Department or Function Managers determine what tasks need to be performed by their Department staff in order to successfully execute the plans assigned to them. Each of these tasks is a series of processes that department staff carries out.

For example, new product development involves several short and medium term steps, from doing market research, to preparing prototypes, to actually launching the product. Each process can have a serious impact on the bottom line, such as making a significant error in recording development costs. Financial controls must ensure that all the appropriate costs associated with developing a new product are recorded to avoid a material misstatement of the financial statements.

2) Listing of processes for achieving Department or Function goals

A list of processes necessary to accomplishing Department tasks is developed. These processes are then broken down to their simplest elements so that they can be mapped out.

Although this is tedious work, it is necessary to document all the processes to become Sarbanes-Oxley compliant. Although the people who actually do the work every day participate, consultants familiar with the particular function usually perform the actual job of recording the steps in the process. Without this documentation, the CEO and CFO cannot be sure that all risks associated with each process have been evaluated.

For example, in the accounts receivable department, each step in recording the receipt of customer account payments involves several steps and each of those steps needs to be documented so that the risk of producing an error on the financial statements can be evaluated.

Department or Function Steps

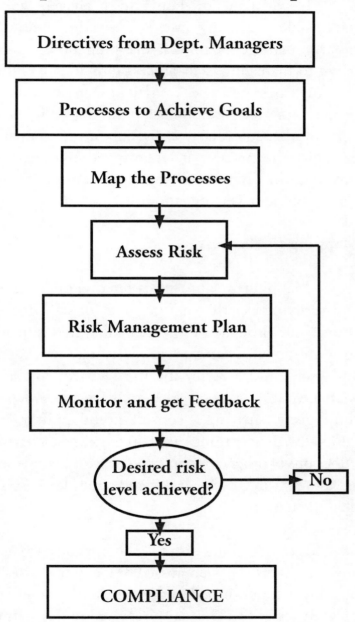

Within Each Process

Department or Function Managers are often responsible for many tasks within their group. It is easier to manage the process-mapping job if it is broken down to managing each process individually. However, in many cases, processes overlap and cross over to other people in a group, another department or function, or even another subsidiary or division of the company. For example, the process of recording the correct cost of inventory involves not only the accounting group, but also shipping, receiving, and other groups.

Mapping the Process

Mapping each process is a matter of documenting and verifying exactly what department staff does in the course of their regular duties. The first step is to get staff to write down what they do every day, week, month, and year. After a review by the Department/Function Manager, it is a good idea to have an independent third party, such as a consultant or auditor, who is familiar with how things work in the same Departments/Functions of other companies, to provide an independent assessment of the accuracy and completeness of the documentation.

It is sometimes easier for an outside party to see if any processes have been missed or if any processes might possibly be performed more efficiently or effectively or with less risk. The day-to-day activities within the department may be so familiar to department staff that some processes may be taken for granted and not included in the documentation.

Assessment of the Risk of Misstatement

For each Department/Function process that has been fully documented, the risk of that process resulting in a material error on the financial statements has to be evaluated. This means measuring the extent to which using that process might lead to an error on the financial statements. For example, if the company needs to back up its data every day, it needs to evaluate the method it uses and decide if the risk of losing the information poses a serious threat to the company's ability to produce accurate financial statements in case of a disaster. If it poses more than a remote chance of creating materially inaccurate financial statements, then this is a material weakness in the financial controls. Steps need to be taken to reduce the risk to an acceptable level. For example, making two back up copies stored in different locations might be sufficient.

Each step in the process has to be examined to see how it could possibly lead to an error, either through unintentional mistakes or by being susceptible to fraudulent manipulation. In other words, the question that must always be asked is: How can it go wrong and how could someone hide it?

Likelihood and Impact

Two elements of the risk of producing a financial statement error (called a misstatement) associated with each process need to be examined. First, the possibility or likelihood that an error will occur must be assessed. Second, if that error does occur, the extent of the effect of that error on the financial statements must also be evaluated. In other words, an informed and educated guess must be made as to how probable it is that there might be an error and how serious it would be if there is an error.

Using Qualitative and Quantitative Methods

Both qualitative and quantitative methods are used to assign a level or risk for each process. Qualitative methods document the nature and cause of events while quantitative methods analyze them numerically. For example, for a large company, a qualitative approach could include an analysis of the political stability of the countries in which it operates. This kind of assessment is obviously subjective and does not lend itself to being quantified. On the other hand, the impact of the different tax systems in each of those countries can easily be measured. For smaller companies, qualitative methods might include an evaluation of the risk of managers having to wear different hats in a small organization. Quantitative methods might involve measuring the impact of paying for increased employment benefits as the company grows.

Establishing a Risk Management Plan

Once the likelihood and impact of possible errors is established for a given process, a priority must be assigned to mitigating the risk associated with that process using available resources. The first step is to set priorities.

Priorities

Those processes with both the highest likelihood of resulting in an error and having the most serious impact on financial statements must be addressed first.

Then, those errors with a low likelihood of occurring, but whose impact would be the greatest, must be balanced against those with a higher possibility of occurring but with a lower impact.

Finally, those with both a low probability of occurring and having a low impact should be assigned the lowest priority. For example, if the company is involved in a large patent infringement court case, and legal counsel says that the company will probably lose, then this is a high priority item because its impact on the company's financial statement will be material. Financial controls must closely monitor the situation and ensure that the liability is correctly recorded and disclosed. On the other hand, the company's process for daily building maintenance is obviously lower priority process because the risk of producing significant errors on the financial statements is remote and its impact small.

Risk Management Plan

Once the risk priorities have been established for each process, a risk management plan for that process must be developed and implemented to reduce the risk of producing a material error in the financial statements.

Because each risk management action plan is unique to each process and its associated risk of producing an error, it must be monitored individually. This is where the concept of financial controls is introduced by the Sarbanes-Oxley Act of 2002.

Financial Controls

Financial controls are the basis of every risk management plan for each of the company's processes. The Act requires that the CEO and the CFO attest yearly as to the effectiveness of their company's financial controls. These financial controls are intended to make sure that the financial statements do not contain serious errors that are referred to as material misstatements.

Monitoring and Feedback

Having effective financial controls means getting feedback to make sure everything works the way it should. Monitoring and feedback are what give the CEO and the CFO assurance that the financial controls are actually working.

Testing the financial controls involves trying to circumvent them. For example, a test could include attempting to make unauthorized changes in the sales figures. The financial controls should prevent these false sales numbers from getting onto the financial statements. Regular verification and spot checks should be part of the financial control process. The company should set up financial controls that are appropriate for each process to ensure that no material errors creep into the financial statements.

Evaluation

If the risk associated with a particular process has more than a remote chance of resulting in a material error on the financial statements, then the company must tighten up the controls and test again.

If the risk associated with a particular process has less than a remote chance of resulting in a material error on the financial statements, it becomes acceptable and that process is compliant with the Sarbanes-Oxley Act of 2002.

Maintaining Compliance

Consistently using this process to assess, evaluate, and control risk within an organization, regardless of the goals of the company, is the key to achieving and maintaining compliance with Section 404 of the Sarbanes-Oxley Act of 2002.

Evaluating and adjusting a company's internal controls is an ongoing process. Following the financial controls compliance process consistently will result in compliance. Reviewing the process, especially through the use of outside consultants, can create opportunities for process improvements. In addition to reducing the risk of producing an error, perhaps there is a better way of doing things.

A Note on the COSO Framework

Many companies use the COSO (Committee of Sponsoring Organizations of the Treadway Commission) framework as an additional guide for evaluating the adequacy of their internal financial controls. COSO was formed in 1985 by 5 major associations in the United States, including the American Institute of Certified Public Accountants and the Institute of Internal Auditors.

The COSO framework was developed to help internal auditors standardize the auditing process for internal controls. It is entirely voluntary and was intended as a guideline for internal company auditors.

The COSO framework is close, but not nearly as demanding a standard as Sarbanes-Oxley. COSO requires only that there be "reasonable assurance" about eliminating the risk of fraud and the reliability of financial reporting. On the other hand, Sarbanes-Oxley focuses on reducing the risk of any material misstatement in the financial statements to only a "remote" chance.

More information on COSO can be found at:

www.coso.org

Chapter 7 Summary

• Section 404 of the Act requires companies to document the internal controls that they use to ensure the accuracy of their financial reports. It requires companies to identify key business processes, the controls overriding the processes, and any vulnerability in these controls.

• Financial controls start at the top and must trickle down. The Board has a mandate from shareholders to provide the best possible return on their investment. The Board sets broad, strategic goals for the company but should leave the day-to-day running the company to the CEO and Senior Management. Senior Management in turn delegates to Middle Management for executing the operational plans by Department or Function.

• Department or Function Managers determine what tasks need to be performed by their Department staff in order to successfully execute the plans assigned to them. A list of processes necessary to accomplishing Department tasks is developed. These processes are then broken down to their simplest elements.

• For each process that has been fully documented, evaluate the risk of that process resulting in a material error.

• Both qualitative and quantitative methods are used to assign a level or risk for each process. Qualitative methods document the nature and cause of events while quantitative methods analyze them numerically.

• Set priorities for modifying processes. Those processes with both the highest likelihood of resulting in an error and having the most serious impact on financial statements must be addressed first,

• Monitoring and feedback prove that the controls are actually working. Testing involves trying to circumvent the controls.

Information Technology 8

Documentation for Compliance

The Sarbanes-Oxley Act of 2002 says that CEO's and CFO's must provide an opinion about the effectiveness of their company's financial controls. In order to comply, companies use information technology (IT) to gather, sort, report, analyze, and communicate information. At the same time, IT provides executives with documentary evidence that financial controls are actually working, and points out any material weaknesses that need to be addressed. Without proper documentation provided by the IT department, CEO's and CFO's would have no basis for expressing an opinion about the effectiveness of their company's financial controls.

IT Crosses All Boundaries

IT is a tool that everyone in the company uses, including the Board, Management, and staff. In addition to communicating information internally, IT is used to communicate with shareholders, customers, suppliers, financial institutions, lenders, regulators, and auditors, among others.

Information Flows Internally In All Directions

Within the organization, the flow of information is up, down and sideways. For example, the Board gives information to Senior Management who in turn passes it on to the Managers. The information is continually fed back to ensure controls are in place. It also flows back and forth sideways across departments and functions. Information technology touches every area of the company so it is an integral and critical part of the financial control process.

The Priority of IT Controls

Since IT is critical to the proper documentation of all other financial controls, setting up the financial controls for IT should be the first step.

Controls for Sensitive Information

Everyone in the company relies on IT to get their job done, from communicating with suppliers and customers, to providing reports up the chain of command. Therefore, people in IT are often placed in positions of trust with confidential, personal, and often time-sensitive information. Because IT employees are privy to confidential information, companies need to set controls over that information.

Applying the Controls Risk Process

Each process in which IT is involved needs to be examined. Once the process has been documented, the probability and impact of an error, whether malicious or not, needs to be evaluated. Priorities are then established in order to deal with the highest risk and the highest impact items first. Resources are allocated appropriately after drawing up a risk management action plan. Using the risk management plan, controls are then put in place that ensure IT issues, deliberate or not, will not produce material misstatements on the financial statements of the company.

Testing of the controls is critical since IT will be the primary tool by which to manage other departments' financial controls. For example, IT manages the levels of access granted to staff for financial information reports. Controls need to be in place to control the criteria used by IT to hand out that access, such as the ability to modify information contained in reports.

Electronic Approvals

Large public companies that span the globe, and have many divisions and many products, require hundreds, if not thousands, of approvals by managers. In order to facilitate the process and reduce the time spent by managers reviewing approvals, many large public companies have introduced, to a certain extent, the automation of the approval process, usually in an electronic form. Larger and less frequent approvals are usually backed up with hardcopy documentation that require the personal signature of the approving manager.

Not only does the approval process itself need to be documented and its risk evaluated, but the underlying IT process must also undergo the same scrutiny, documentation, and risk evaluation. For example, if the approval process relies on a form that needs to be filled out by the requesting employee, and subsequently approved by manager, IT controls must ensure that the form cannot be altered at any step in the process except by those who are authorized to make those changes. Thus, IT controls form an integral and critical part of the controls for approvals.

Controls for Hardware and Software

Strict controls for hardware need to be implemented and maintained. For example, when a computer meets be repaired or replaced, there needs to be controls for IT that ensure that the company information is not lost or does not fall into the wrong hands, whether deliberate or not. The controls must ensure that the information cannot be altered, especially if it is used to produce information that will ultimately become part of the financial statements. For example, if a computer is sent out for repair, there must be arrangements made beforehand and controls in place to assure that the information cannot be altered while out of the company's hands. Better yet, there should be a process in place to remove all the information off the computer before it leaves the department.

Spreadsheets

The same strict controls must exist for software. For example, finance departments make extensive use of spreadsheet software such as Microsoft's Excel. The spreadsheets companies use for reporting must have controls in place that:

1) limit access to these spreadsheets,
2) control who can change information,
3) control which employees can add or delete information,
4) controls who must approve the use
5) regulates how the information will be stored so that it will be safeguarded.

For example, one level of staff may be responsible for gathering and transferring inventory information into spreadsheets, but they would not be able to modify or delete the information once it has been entered into the spreadsheet. Only those with specific authority should be able to make any changes or delete entries. This protects the information from fraudulent tampering to some extent.

Laptop Computers

Financial controls for laptop computers, especially those that are routinely taken home by employees, are critical. Access must be strictly limited to employees authorized to do so. Controls must make sure that no one can remove the laptop from the office without authorization. In addition, IT controls must be put in place that will ensure that the data on any laptop or desk computer cannot be accessed, and that the data on those computers cannot be altered in any way in an attempt to hide fraud by erasing or substituting information.

Protection should be built into laptops to protect their information in the event that they are stolen. Unfortunately, the difficulty of protecting data only via passwords is that software can get around password protection. It needs to be "hard-wired" in and that can become cumbersome, expensive, and not nearly as reliable as people want to believe. It is much better to restrict the type of information that can be put on laptops so that it cannot leave the building.

Another issue is the growing trend toward wireless technology. Since this is a relatively new phenomenon, the jury is still out as to whether information transmitted this way can be protected 100%. To be on the safe side, some companies have chosen to ban the use of wireless technology to access company networks.

Network Administration

Network administration is an area that requires strong controls to protect the integrity of financial information by preventing anyone, whether they are inside or outside the company, from accessing information without proper authorization. There is always a danger that employees will try to access or change information to hide fraud.

Controls should prevent people who do have access from changing information that should not be changed. For example, a finance employee should not be able to access company financial reports except those to which that finance employee has been granted specific access, or they may have restricted access to only read information but not change it. There should be no opportunity for such an employee to modify information that would lead to a material misstatement on the company's financial statements. The employee may be simply trying to cover up a silly mistake he or she made earlier, or it may be something more sinister, such as industrial espionage.

Limiting access includes not only internal employee limits to information, but also includes strong controls to prevent access by unauthorized parties outside the company. For example, people with malicious intentions cannot be allowed to hack into the company's computer system to alter information. These controls must be documented and tested regularly. Executives have a responsibility to safeguard the company's critical information.

Backup

All companies need to back up the IT information stored in their computers. Controls need to virtually guarantee that those financial statements can be reproduced faithfully in the event of a disaster. Those same controls must be able to document how the company executives can be assured that the backup copies are the same as the original information. For example, the controls need to keep track of who is doing the backup, the source of the information that is backed up, how it is stored, how it is protected, how is retrieved, how it is reproduced, and how often the backup is done.

A good test of the controls would be to simulate a disaster and track how successful the controls were at limiting risk and producing the desired results.

Audit Trails

IT controls play a vital role in the audit process by providing audit trails. Not only are they useful for confirming the effectiveness of financial controls, but they can be extremely useful in discovering fraud. For example, tracking down small, but frequent inventory losses can point to an inadequate tracking system or, at worst, a dishonest employee.

Safeguarding Personal Information

A growing issue with many companies is the protection of personal information received from their customers. Although privacy legislation varies from country to country, it is simply good business to protect private client information. Controls need to virtually eliminate the risk of private client information being lost or falling into the wrong hands.

Privacy laws such as those in Europe and in Canada (PIPEDA) strictly control the collection, use, and disclosure of consumer's personal information. The safeguarding of information is a key function of IT and its failure can open up the company to expensive lawsuits.

It is simply good business to protect customer information. If a client loses confidence in the company's ability to protect their information, they may take their business elsewhere. This will adversely affect the company's revenue and reputation, and will be reflected in the financial statements.

Chapter 8 Summary

• Companies use information technology (IT) to gather, sort, report, analyze, and communicate information. At the same time, IT provides executives with documentary evidence that financial controls are actually working, and points out any material weaknesses that need to be addressed.

• Since information technology is critical to the proper documentation of all other financial controls, setting up the financial controls for IT should be the first step.

• Employees in IT are in positions of trust involving confidential, personal, and often time-sensitive information. Since they are privy to so much confidential information, companies need to set controls over that information.

• Large public companies that have many divisions and many products require hundreds of approvals by managers. To facilitate the process and reduce the time spent by managers reviewing approvals, many companies have introduced the automation of the approval process in an electronic form.

• Strict controls for hardware and software need to be implemented and maintained to prevent unauthorized access to confidential information.

• Network access must be strictly controlled.

• All companies need to back up the information stored in their computers. Controls need to guarantee that those financial statements can be reproduced faithfully in the event of a disaster.

• Privacy laws strictly control the collection, use, and disclosure of consumer's personal information. The failure to safeguard personal information can open up the company to expensive lawsuits.

Inventory

9

Risk of Manipulation

Inventory is one area that lends itself more easily to manipulation than other areas. Inventory can be hidden, stolen, or simply forgotten. Weak controls can pose a serious risk of material misstatements on the company's financial statements.

Determining Accountability for Inventory

The first step in creating financial controls for inventory starts with determining accountability for inventory. Defining and documenting exactly who is responsible for inventory is not quite as easy as it sounds.

Inventory doesn't start out as inventory. It starts out as a purchase order, becomes an order to the supplier, a received shipment, is stored, in a manufacturing environment it becomes work in process, is prepared for shipment, and delivered to the customer. At every stage different people are responsible for this company asset called inventory. Each stage follows a different process, or series of processes to accomplish the tasks assigned to them.

Each of these processes needs to be documented and evaluated in terms of what the risks are of producing an error on the financial statements. For example, the original decision to purchase the inventory often stems from a customer order that is usually handled by the sales group. Documenting the process of receiving a customer order is the first step in assessing the risk of accepting and filling the order. The sales group hands it off to purchasing who will proceed with finding and securing the necessary materials, which may pose some risk if it cannot be done in time or if the items are not of sufficient quality. These are all risks that must be controlled and can have an impact on the financial statements.

Since inventory is often the largest or second-largest asset on a company's balance sheet, the processes related to inventory are important because of their large potential impact on the balance sheet. So the processes of documenting, evaluating, establishing, and monitoring the risks associated with inventory should have a high priority when it comes to allocating resources for Sarbanes-Oxley compliance tasks.

Obsolescence

The treatment of inventory obsolescence is a process that requires tight financial controls because an error can have a significant impact on the company's financial statements. Writing off obsolete inventory can be a significant expense.

This is an area where the potential for fraud is great. These write-offs of inventory were common when they appeared as one-time charges during the high-tech boom years. These one-time charges were used to even out the profit figures over several quarters so that investors could be fooled into thinking the company was on a steady climb to more profits. For example, if profits were not good for a given quarter, companies would wait for a good quarter to take the write-offs to take the one-time charge. This gave the false impression that profits were on a steady climb, to attract and keep investors.

On the other hand, carrying inventory at an over-inflated value can lead to understated expenses and overstated profits. Again an area with tremendous potential for fraud, so having tight controls to ensure that the correct inventory figure is reported is absolutely critical. Every step in the process, including approvals for write-downs, must be documented. The risk of an error needs to be eliminated. Employees, such as purchasing managers, who have a vested interest in not writing down inventory because it would highlight their poor buying decisions, should not be the people responsible for writing off obsolete inventory. At the very least, the write-off needs to be approved by finance.

Here is another example of a possibility of fraud if the controls are weak. When companies are looking for financing, the lender will often request that the inventory be used as collateral for the loan and that the amount of the ongoing financing be tied to the level of inventory. Usually, there will be a covenant that the loan must be paid down if the inventory value falls. Companies can make themselves look better by not writing down obsolete inventory. Financial controls that eliminate that risk will help to ensure that the company abides by its loan covenants.

Valuation

Valuation of inventory is an area that requires good financial controls. Having good controls requires having good documentation. Valuations require good market information, including competitor prices, to correctly reflect the value of inventory in the financial statements. Controls need to set up to verify the information on which the valuation is based. They also must be able to catch any attempted fraud by unscrupulous employees trying to cover theft of inventory.

Inventory Sent to Outside Processors

When inventory is sent out from the company's

premises for any processing, such as outside assemblers, documentation is vital to financial controls for inventory. The company executives need to make sure that all inventories are accounted for. This is yet another area where the potential for fraud is great. Controls have to be in place to catch any "shrinkage" so that any collusion between company employees and the outsource company will be caught.

A Sale That Is Not a Sale

Financial controls need to be set up to catch a practice that was all too common during the high tech boom. The practice of invoicing customers at month-end, recognizing the sale, and then issuing a credit for the return of the goods to the supplier after month-end was widespread. Companies benefited from this game by inflating sales figures and reporting their investment in inventory as lower than it actually was. It was bad for investors and banks because not only did it produce a false income statement and balance sheet, but also the cash flow relied upon by investors and lenders did not exist. The Accounts Receivable reported from the non-existent sale would never be turned into cash. Only a credit note would be issued. Reduced cash meant a reduced ability to pay dividends or accounts payable.

The inventory going back and forth eventually became obsolete and a significant write-down would be taken in some future quarter when it was hoped that profits would be able to cover up some of the losses.

It is virtually certain that the company executives were well aware of the fraud that was taking place but either chose to ignore it or actually encouraged the practice. Since they did not have to personally certify the financial statements and attest to the effectiveness of their company's financial controls the personal risk to them was insignificant compared to the potential gains in the company's stock price.

Inventory Leaving the Premises

Financial controls for documenting any inventory leaving the company premises need to be well established. For example, samples being taken out by the sales group need to be tracked. They can add up and have a significant impact on the financial statements.

Inventory Counts

Because inventory often represents a significant part a company's balance sheet, inventory counts need to be well controlled. Staff that may try to cover up theft by falsifying inventory count information. Good controls will provide the company with information about inventory that never actually arrived or inventory that has been stolen and sold by dishonest staff.

Supervision of the count should be completely out of the hands of the people who are responsible for the inventory. Any shortfalls need to be investigated and the root cause uncovered. For example, strong controls for recording inventory purchases and the receipt of merchandise will help the company track down any theft of inventory.

The financial controls for inventory counts are critical because they can lead to many other areas that may contain financial risk. For example, if a count uncovers a problem from inventory that has become spoiled because the warehouse is not sufficiently heated, the risk of loss due to poor warehouse maintenance will be highlighted and can be immediately addressed.

Chapter 9 Summary

• The first step in creating financial controls for inventory starts with determining accountability for inventory.

• Writing off obsolete inventory is an area where the potential for fraudulently manipulating numbers is great.

• Inventory valuation is another area that is vulnerable to manipulation. Valuations require good market information, including competitor prices, to correctly reflect the value of inventory in the financial statements.

• A Sale That Is Not A Sale. The practice of invoicing customers at month-end, recognizing the sale, and then issuing a credit for the return of the goods to the supplier after month-end was a widespread practice which will no longer be tolerated by either investors or auditors.

• To limit the likelihood of fraud, supervision of inventory counts should be completely out of the hands of the people who are responsible for the inventory.

Accounts Receivable

10

For many companies, Accounts Receivable is the largest or second-largest asset on their balance sheet. Therefore, any weakness in the financial controls for Accounts Receivable could have a serious impact on the company's financial statements. Since Accounts Receivable departments interact with almost every other department in the company, the Accounts Receivable processes affect almost every process in the company. Weak controls can lead to increased risk in many other areas.

The Sales Contract

Every Account Receivable is a result of a sale. Accounts Receivable employees are in the business of converting Accounts Receivable into Cash. In order to be truly an Account Receivable, the sale must be based on a valid sales contract. Every sale must be based on a sales contract, whether it is the same sales agreement for all customers, or whether a unique contract has been drawn up for a particular sale.

Collecting Before You Sell

The collection process should start even before the sale is made, even before the sales department goes after a particular customer. Accounts Receivable processes can reduce the risk of dealing with a particular customer by pre-qualifying customers as much as possible.

It is better to not make the sale than to make a sale that you cannot collect. For example, if your profit on a particular item is 5% and you cannot collect then you are much worse off than if you hadn't made the sale. If the sale price is $100, and the profit is 5%, then the company makes $5. However, if the sale is on credit and the Account Receivable amount of $100 is written off to bad debt, then it takes 20 additional sales or $2000 to recover the $100 write-off. Every process in Accounts Receivable that prevents a write-off in a 5% profit margin environment is equal to 20 sales. Accounts Receivable processes that work well are extremely valuable.

Accounts Receivable should be involved in the drawing up of the sales agreement because this document will have a serious impact on the company's ability to collect, and ultimately a serious impact on the company's financial statement.

Controlling the documentation received from the customer is critical to successfully converting Accounts Receivable to cash and avoiding having to write off bad debts. Weak controls in this area can have a serious impact. The controls need to work because the risk of not following through and producing a misstatement can be high. For example, shipping products to a customer without first obtaining the proper approvals for the sales contract can mean that the company will not get paid. If the contract was thought to provide security in case of non-payment, but if someone who was supposed to review the deal did not catch a defect in the document, those Accounts Receivable dollars may be in jeopardy. As a result, a reserve for doubtful accounts needs to be established for the Account Receivable, thus reducing profits substantially. If not, the Accounts Receivable figure will be overstated and the company's financial statements will contain a material misstatement.

Terms

Accounts Receivable payment terms need to be clearly spelled out. The Accounts Receivable financial controls need to be able to catch all deviations from the established processes. They also need to spell out the approval process, including who has the authority to approve credit.

Sales should never have the final say in approving credit. Their input is always welcome, but the authority and responsibility for approving credit should reside inside the credit department. Controls within the company need to prevent unauthorized shipments (not credit approved) to customers. For example, shipping on consignment terms instead of open terms requires different documentation and processes. Financial controls have to be in place to reduce the risk of an error in documentation. The financial statements must reflect the true risk of the particular Account Receivable. The company should not report the Account Receivable as collectable when in fact a defective document may prove to be worthless when it comes time to enforce collection.

Sales Returns

The process of recording customer sales returns of inventory needs to be included in the Accounts Receivable financial controls. When a customer returns goods, the inventory needs to be recorded back into the company's balance sheet. At the same time, a credit note should be issued to reduce the amount collectible from the customer. Controls need to ensure that the company is not carrying on its books Accounts Receivable that is not waiting to be collected, but instead is waiting to be eliminated by a credit note to the customer's account.

Companies often have poor controls in this area. If sales or customer service departments are responsible for issuing credit notes, they will often drag their feet because the sales activities have a higher priority, or they may simply not want to reduce their sales figure until after month end or year-end.

The amount of the credit note issued may actually

be more or it may be less than anticipated. For example, because there may be clauses in the sales agreement that stipulate that the company, not the customer, will pay for shipping charges, the credit will be more. On the other hand, the sales agreement may say that the company can charge a "restocking fee" when material is returned, which will reduce the amount of the credit note.

Each clause in the sales agreement needs to be examined and the risk associated with it evaluated and controls put in place to reduce that risk.

Companies need to strengthen their financial controls to ensure that Accounts Receivable is not materially overstated because of pending sales return credit notes.

Interest

If the financial controls over Accounts Receivable are weak, then the controls over the process of charging interest to overdue customers may also be weak. Since interest is based on the interest provision of the original sales agreement, financial controls must ensure that overdue interest is charged according to the contract. For example, one customer may be given 60 days to pay while another may have to pay in 30 days. Charging interest on all overdue customer accounts that are over 30 days old would not be correct. The amount of interest recorded in the financial statements would not reflect the company's legal right to collect that interest. Financial controls need to make sure that every dollar of interest on the books is justified.

The Collection Process

The collection process itself needs to be tightly controlled. Obviously, if some of the Accounts Receivable staff does not follow the established process for collecting accounts, they may not collect some of the company's money and significant amounts may have to be written off. Controls need to be in place that reduces risk by ensuring that collectors follow established collection policy.

There is more risk than most people are aware of in the collection process. If the management controls for the process itself are weak, the way collectors do their job could mean that rather than collecting money, the company may be at risk of being fined or sued from following unscrupulous, if not downright illegal, collection practices. For example, if the collection staff is taking a customer to court in attempt to collect, they company may end up being sued by the customer if it is a frivolous suit. An obvious and simple control would be to require prior approval by management before this step is taken. Not only would it reduce the risk of a counter-suit, but also it would eliminate unnecessary costs and frustration. Financial controls that require the proper management approvals will prevent things from getting that far.

Collecting from consumers is very different from collecting from businesses. The laws governing collection action and deadlines, security and privacy are different. Companies need to have financial controls to make sure that all legal requirements are met and that opportunities for collection are not lost because of weak controls.

Time-Sensitive Documents

Financial controls of time-sensitive documents used as collateral are critical because the huge impact they may have on the company's financial statements. For example, if the company is counting on a letter of credit to back up their decision to grant credit, a collector who does not follow the process may lose the chance to collect the money if he or she does not act before the letter of credit expires. Another example is losing lien rights because someone forgot to renew it before the expiry date.

Setting Credit Limits

Setting the proper credit limits is critical to good Accounts Receivable management. The criteria used to set limits, the investigative process, and the approval limit hierarchy must be clearly spelled out in the Accounts Receivable financial controls, which should include a written credit policy.

This area requires special attention because the setting of credit limits should be very deliberate.

Choosing the correct limit should be a result of following a clearly prescribed process that should be easily followed and the result easily duplicated. For example, if two different credit analysts were to work independently on setting a credit limit using exactly the same information, they should arrive at the same recommendation, within a narrow range, if they follow the same process. Controls should ensure that analysts would consistently arrive at the same result.

Another control that companies use is to have credit approval limits for each member of the credit department. The greater the risk (the more money involved), the higher up the chain of command approval is required. For example, a credit analyst may be able to approve limits up to $50,000, the credit manager up to $100,000, the VP Finance up to $500,000 and the CEO must approve all limits above $500,000.

Credit Scoring

The advent of credit scoring to speed up the credit approval process has a built in risk that needs to be assessed and carefully controlled. The use of these models means sacrificing individual assessments that may take more time and be more costly. The benefit of faster response time in a competitive environment may be cost effective for companies who increase their profits by more than the amount of bad debt they will write-off using this system. However, a strong control and monitoring process coupled with a continual testing of the underlying assumptions of the scoring model is needed to assure the company that the risks are being controlled adequately. For example, the model might assume that all customers who have been in business at least ten years should be scored higher than those that have been in business a shorter time. The test is how old are the businesses whose accounts get written off. If how long they have been in business does not seem to be a factor, then the model and the risk associated with it need to be reassessed.

Outsourcing

Companies that outsource any of the Credit and Accounts Receivable functions need to set up strong financial controls to ensure that the outsource companies actually do what they promise to do. For example, if the credit application process involves sending the electronic application form out to a third party to do preliminary, routine verifications of the corporate name and banking information, there is a risk that these companies may not do a thorough job in all cases. This risk must be evaluated and controlled so that the company knows who they are dealing with. A small error here could mean an inability to collect because the invoices are invoiced to the wrong company, and the assets that were thought to be available in case of a collection problem actually belong to another corporation.

Collection Agencies

Sending accounts to collection agencies requires that someone monitor their efforts. Strong financial controls here can retrieve cash that would not have come in if the collection agencies were not being monitored. For example, if they can get away with it, collection agencies will only work larger accounts because they are paid a commission (usually a third to a half) of the amount they collect. Therefore, they tend to work large accounts and leave the smaller ones for later. Letting the collection agencies get away with this means letting your smaller accounts get old and they are less likely to be collected as time goes on. Collection agencies will be less inclined to try this if they know that you have controls to monitor their performance. Stay on top of the situation and demand that they work both large and small accounts. The process needs to be documented, examined, and the risk associated with it evaluated and controlled. Your monitoring will reveal if you are not getting the performance that you demand from the collection agency and you will know when it is time to move the accounts.

Monitoring Customer Creditworthiness

Controls need to be in place to monitor, on an ongoing basis, the creditworthiness of customers. The process has to be clearly proactive to get ahead of any deterioration in a customer's ability to pay their bills on time. Otherwise waiting for the moment when the customer cannot pay will lead to a high risk of never getting paid.

Criteria need to be established to alert staff to begin a credit investigation. Other than a late payment, triggers for an investigation before their regular review can be any change in pattern such as an increase in deductions, a number of excuses for delays in payments, asking for copies of invoices to delay payment, calls not being returned and, of course, the old standby that the person who needs to approve the payment is away.

If there is no process established to manage this risk, the controls are weak and this is an area where Management must disclose in its report this weakness in their financial controls.

Controls for the Acceptance of Collateral

When collateral is required to approve credit, such as a stand-by letter of credit, financial controls should ensure that the documentation is valid before shipping to a customer or providing a service. For example, the controls may require that the credit department obtain a sign-off from the Legal Department to make sure the document can be relied upon if it becomes necessary to use the letter of credit to collect. It may also say that the Treasury Department must approve the choice of financial institutions on which the letter of credit is drawn.

Weak controls in this area could produce of substantial risk of not being able to collect and a huge impact on the company's financial statement.

Bad Debt Allowance

The allowance for bad debt is an account that needs strong financial controls. The approval process, along with the criteria for inclusion, is a process that can lend itself to manipulation if it is not tightly controlled.

Too many companies use this account to even out bumps in the income statement from quarter to quarter. Companies will "pad" the bad debt allowance account in good years and pull it back in lean years.

This is a poor practice because the amount of the allowance should be a reflection of the level of "collectibility" of Accounts Receivable. The goal is to state Accounts Receivable at its "net realizable value." In other words, it should be the amount of cash the company is expected to actually collect. Otherwise, the allowance is wrong and the expense will cause the profit number to be wrong. The company will also have to report this control weakness on their annual report in order to be Sarbanes-Oxley compliant.

Write-offs

As much as Accounts Receivable people try to avoid them, bad debt write-offs are a part of doing business on credit terms. Financial controls need to be in place that set out the process for identifying, documenting, and approving bad debt write-offs. Look at every step in the process to see if it poses a risk of producing an error on the financial statement. For example, financial controls should stipulate that the larger the amount of the write-off, the higher up the chain of command it has to go to be approved.

Deductions

Financial controls need to be in place for when customers take deductions from their invoices. These deductions can be for things such as poor quality, wrong product shipped, wrong price, shipped to the wrong location, wrong quantity shipped, and billed on the wrong purchase order. Customers will pay only for exactly what they ordered.

Controls need to manage how these disputes are resolved and who is responsible for getting them resolved. Although the balance is on the customer's account and therefore is ultimately up to Accounts Receivable to make sure it is dealt with, the resolution will often rest outside the Accounts Receivable area. For example, if a customer is refusing to pay because they believe the price is wrong, the invoicing people need to either correct the wrong invoice or confirm to the Accounts Receivable people that the invoice price is correct as billed. Until that confirmation is received from the Billing Department, Accounts Receivable cannot proceed with collection action because of the pending dispute. Strong financial controls and clear processes need to reduce the risk of the amount of Accounts Receivable deductions on the books having a serious impact on the company's financial statements.

Risk Imported from other Departments or Functions

Since many processes in Accounts Receivable depend on other departments or functions, the risks associated with those processes can affect Accounts Receivable. Therefore, documenting and assessing their risk of the processes in other departments that are pertinent to Accounts Receivable is required to become Sarbanes-Oxley compliant.

Because Accounts Receivable processes involve sales, shipping, customer service, receiving, finance, inventory control, purchasing, and many others, the risks of the processes in other departments have to be taken into account when evaluating the processes in the Accounts Receivable department. This level of integration requires strong financial controls and a clear understanding of the impact other department processes on the Accounts Receivable risk.

Collusion

Financial controls should be set up to catch any collusion among employees, especially in Accounts Receivable. The best control is a strong separation of duties. For example, the person who is responsible for applying the payments to customer accounts should not have the authority to write off small amounts. Someone else should approve these. If these two are working together to defraud the company, a regular review of all small write-offs should be the responsibility of a third person, preferably outside Accounts Receivable, such as in Accounting or Finance.

Chapter 10 Summary

• For many companies, Accounts Receivable is the largest or second-largest asset on their balance sheet. Therefore, any weakness in the financial controls for Accounts Receivable could have a serious impact on the company's financial statements.

• Accounts Receivable should be involved in the drawing up of the sales agreement right from the start. Controlling the documentation received from the customer is critical to successfully converting Accounts Receivable to cash and avoiding having to write off bad debts.

• Controls need to be in place to prevent unauthorized shipments (not credit approved) to customers.

• The process of recording customer sales returns is one area where companies often have poor controls. If sales or customer service departments are responsible for issuing credit notes, they will often drag their feet because the sales activities have a higher priority, or they may simply not want to reduce their sales figure until after month end or year-end.

• The collection process itself needs to be tightly controlled. If Accounts Receivable staff does not follow the established process for collecting accounts, they may be unable to collect and significant amounts may have to be written off.

• Determining credit limits should be the result of following a clearly prescribed process that is easy to follow and the result easily duplicated. If two different credit analysts were to work independently on setting a credit limit using exactly the same information, they should arrive at the same recommendation, within a narrow range, if they follow the same process. Controls should ensure that analysts would consistently arrive at the same result.

• Careful monitoring of collection agency performance can retrieve cash that would not have come in if the collection agencies were not being monitored. Collection agencies will tend to work larger accounts because of the larger commission, leaving the smaller ones for later, making them less likely to be collected as time goes on.

• The allowance for bad debt needs strong financial controls. The approval process along with the criteria for inclusion is a process that can lend itself to manipulation if it is not tightly controlled.

• Bad debt write-offs are a part of doing business on credit terms. Financial controls need to be in place that set out the process for identifying, documenting, and approving bad debt write-offs.

• Because many processes in Accounts Receivable depend on other departments or functions, the risks associated with those processes can affect Accounts Receivable.

Accounts Payable

11

Documenting financial controls for Accounts Payable begins with looking at the payments that are processed by a typical large company Accounts Payable department. These payments can include supplier payments, payroll, taxes, building mortgage payments, insurance payments, and miscellaneous payments, such as charitable donations, customer deposit refunds, and consulting fees.

Inventory Purchasing/Supplier Payments

Supplier payments start with the company's purchasing department. Documenting the purchasing process and analyzing the risk to the financial statements is a daunting task, given the many different items a large company has to purchase every day. However, this is an area where there is tremendous opportunity for fraud. Controls must be able to detect when the appropriate approvals have not been obtained and prevent any material amounts from contaminating the financial statements. It need not be just one large amount. It can be numerous small amounts whose cumulative effect is material.

Here is an example of a control mechanism for Accounts Payable. Many companies require that a purchase order to be drawn up for every purchase. That purchase order must be approved by the requesting department manager and by the purchasing department. If an invoice is submitted for payment without a reference to the purchase order number, the Accounts Payable department will reject the request and ask that a valid purchase order be submitted. This prevents someone from submitting a false invoice.

In addition, the invoice must match the details on the purchase order such as price and quantity. If it does not, it is rejected and the invoice is not paid. Rejected invoices are submitted to the purchasing department for follow up.

False Invoices

Some companies have instituted a dollar limit control below which supplier invoices do not require the usual approval process. Companies allow them to be "fast-tracked." Criminals can take advantage of this policy and bilk companies for large sums of money. If a company pays all invoices under $100 without the usual process, then invoices for $90 can be submitted over and over again. One example is false magazine subscriptions. They get paid every month, quarter, and year, and can add up to many thousands of dollars. Controls need to be in place to catch these repeat offenders.

Payroll

Payroll controls need to be in place to make sure that payments are not being made to fictitious people. This may sound obvious, but processes need to be examined for all possible risks. Paying people after they have left the company, or who are deceased, is not as infrequent as you may think.

Another process that has potential for significant errors, intentional or not, are time sheets for hourly employees. Controls must catch these errors. A simple but effective example is to have the department manager whose budget will pay for that employee to sign off on the hours worked. This also works well for temporary employees hired through employment agencies.

Taxes

Financial controls need to look at the area of government tax payments. The impact of taxes on the company's financial statements can be significant.

Paying too much, which leads to recording too high an expense for taxes, can be as much of a problem as not paying enough and having to pay unnecessary penalties and litigation costs.

There is also the issue of timing. Financial controls must ensure that time sensitive payments, such as payroll taxes are paid on time and in the correct amount.

Miscellaneous Payments

Unusual or infrequent payments fall into this category. This may include charitable donations or funds for educational support for employees. Financial controls need to make sure these payments have received appropriate approvals, are paid to the correct parties, and that any abuses will be caught.

The company could be operating in a country where bribes are a way of getting things done and are seen as a normal, necessary business expense. However, financial statements of US based companies need to reflect US laws and regulations. Bribes are not an acceptable way of doing business in the United States and controls need to catch any such payments, especially in rolling up financial information from foreign subsidiaries into the consolidated financial statements of the US head office. Many companies simply have a policy of not paying bribes. They would rather forgo the business than participate in illegal activities. Often, the Board of Directors specifies in their directives to the CEO and Senior Management that illegal activities are strictly out of bounds.

Although the Sarbanes-Oxley Act of 2002 does not specifically mention bribes, many companies are choosing not to do business in this manner any longer as a result of the more intense scrutiny on the part of auditors and investors.

Approval Limits

The Accounts Payable financial controls need to include approval limits for all people in the organization, from Board members on down. As the risk increases with the amount to be paid, so should the level and number of approvals. The controls should also spell out the documentation necessary for that approval. Accountability is the key to making these controls work.

The Accounts Payable department needs to have strong financial controls that lets them control all monies before the company pays them out. It is far easier to keep the money than it is to get it back after it has been paid out by mistake.

Types of Approvals

The company must put in place financial controls that specify the type of approval that will be acceptable, given any level of purchase. For example, hardcopy approval on specified documentation should be the requirement for any significant spending. If the amounts are small, and the IT controls are strong, electronic approvals may be sufficient. The risk of electronic approvals needs to be carefully assessed and controlled.

Who can approve and how they can approve is part of the risk assessment in analyzing the Accounts Payable financial controls.

Repetitive Processes

Accounts Payable departments in large public companies deal with thousands, if not millions, of documents. The process of receiving, classifying, approving, paying, and filing these documents is a process that has risk at every step. For example, not paying insurance premiums as they become due may mean the company does not have the coverage it thought it did. If a fire occurs, the insurance payments that the company was relying on would not be received if the premiums were not up to date.

Inter-company Payments

Payments for settling inter-company shipments between divisions located in different geographies or selling different products should not affect the consolidated financial statements because inter-company transactions are netted out. However, there are opportunities for errors to creep into the financial statements if financial controls are weak. For example, if a shipment of inventory is not recorded correctly, or not at all, there is an opportunity for fraud, or, at the very least, recording inventory incorrectly.

Controls need to track inter-company shipments as they leave, in transit, and as they arrive.

Department Managers Holding Invoices

In my experience, some department managers do not process invoices in a timely manner. They get busy and leave processing invoices for later. They do not see approving an invoice for their department as a high priority. They intend to get around to it when things slow down. Financial controls need to make sure all invoices are recorded, and processed for payment in a timely manner. Otherwise, liabilities are not recorded correctly, and the Accounts Payable figure will be incorrect.

Accruals

Another area that lends itself to errors if financial controls are weak is month-end and year-end accruals for Accounts Payable. If all liabilities are not accounted for at the date of the financial statements, obviously the Accounts Payable figure will be wrong. Strong controls need to make sure all company liabilities are reflected in the financial statements. For example, if the supplier invoices for shipments received before year-end are not accrued correctly, financial controls need to catch that. They also should catch any opportunities for fraud in this area.

Other Areas in Accounts Payable

Other areas that require good financial controls include the control of checks, such as making sure all blank check forms are securely stored, and that a process exists for requisitioning and receiving check forms. It goes without saying that there should be no pre-signed checks. All backup documents for taxes need to be stored securely, but be easily retrievable for government audits.

For multi-national companies, controls must ensure that payments are issued in the same currency as the invoice (or the equivalent value). You don't want to pay 4 million US dollars when the bill is 4 million Mexican Pesos.

Finally, audit trails for all payments must be clear, well documented, and easy to follow.

Chapter 11 Summary

• Controls must be able to detect when the appropriate purchasing approvals have not been obtained. Large amounts obviously make a difference, but so do numerous small amounts whose cumulative effect is material.

• Some companies have instituted a dollar limit control below which supplier invoices do not require the usual approval process. Criminals can take advantage of this policy and bilk companies for large sums of money.

• Payroll controls need to be in place to make sure that payments are not being made to fictitious people, or people who are no longer with the company.

• Financial controls need to look at the area of government tax payments. Paying too much, which leads to recording too high an expense for taxes, can be as much of a problem as not paying enough and having to pay unnecessary penalties and litigation costs. Tax payments are often time-sensitive.

• The A/P financial controls need to include approval limits for everyone from Board members on down. As the risk increases with the amount to be paid, so should the level and number of approvals.

• Audit trails for all payments must be clear, well documented, and easy to follow.

Financial Controls for Assets 12

Asset Policies

Effective financial controls should include a good company policy for assets being sold, purchased, or transferred. It should be clear, concise, easy to understand, and communicated to everyone in the company. There should be no doubt about the procedures, and what the consequences will be for not following them.

Valuation

The valuation of assets (the value at which the asset is recorded) can easily lead to errors on the company's financial statements. Overvaluing an asset, such as land, a building, or equipment, means that these assets are overstated, and would mislead investors about the net worth of the company.

Approvals for Purchasing Assets

In large and diverse public companies, approving

the purchase of assets for many divisions and locations worldwide requires strong financial controls. The process must be flexible enough to let the business operate efficiently, yet it must provide prudent risk management. For example, importing items from outside the country may require completely different documentation than buying the items locally. The risk of making a mistake in the required documentation can mean not getting the goods on time to deliver to a customer as promised. Missing the delivery deadline could be expensive and could even mean losing an important sale.

When the Purchase Price is Out of Line

Sarbanes-Oxley requires that internal controls must make sure not only that all assets are accounted for in the financial statements, but also that the price paid and subsequently recorded in the balance sheet is correct. The controls should catch anything that is not right.

If a price is not in keeping with the normal price of similar items, controls should detect it so that it can be investigated. If an invoiced price for the purchase of an asset seems to be out of line with the expected cost there might be a number of explanations.

1) Is it a matter of fraud? For example, perhaps the Facilities Manager contracted with a landscaping company to upgrade the landscaping around the office building and paid an inflated price in exchange for

secretly getting landscaping work done on his home for free. Effective controls in the form of an established bid procurement process would reduce the likelihood of this sort of thing happening.

2) Is it a matter of negligence? For example, perhaps the Facilities Manager neglected to put the job out for bidding and the landscaping contractor took advantage of the situation and inflated the bill. Requiring that all purchases over a specific dollar amount must be put out for bids would prevent this from happening.

3) Or is the price in line with competing bids but just seems high because it has been so long since this sort of asset was last purchased? For example, the last time any landscaping was done was 20 years ago and the prices have risen dramatically. Getting enough competing bids will show that the price is in line.

Other financial controls for the purchase of assets might include requiring documentation of an independent appraisal of the value of the asset and several levels of approval prior to the purchase. As well, the larger the value of the asset being sold or purchased, the higher up the chain of command the approval should go.

Preventing Assets from Walking Out

Small items are particularly susceptible to "walking out the door." In the high tech industry, for example, small electronic items can be very expensive and easy to steal. Good security will help prevent these small but valuable items from being stolen. The inventory loss would reduce the profitability of the company and its net worth if it happens often enough. This does not mean large items cannot walk out as well. People posing as movers have stolen desks, computers, and other large items from companies. Again, good security and asset controls are important in reducing the risk of adversely affecting the financial statements.

Preventing Assets from Being Sold by Staff

Financial controls should catch fraudulent sales by employees. For example, basic security measures should catch warehouse staff that could be selling materials out the back door for cash. Spot checks and rotating staff are also good ideas. If this activity goes unchecked, it can have a negative impact not only on the company's financial statements, but can hurt its reputation and seriously reduce its market share.

Assets for Employees Working Out of the Office

Employees working out of the office, either on the road or at home, often need company assets such as laptops and other communication devices. These need to be secure to protect the company's information. In addition, the assets need to be accounted for. Internal controls need to ensure that these assets actually exist and are in the possession of the employee. The employee could be asked, when practical, to bring in the asset for verification, every six months or yearly.

Intellectual Property

The company's biggest asset, after its employees, is its intellectual property. For this reason, industrial manufacturing secrets should be safeguarded. The risks associated with industrial secrets can be significant. If there is a leak of information and a competitor can duplicate a company's product and sell it at a price that will virtually steal the market away from the company, there is real risk that the company could be driven out of business. These risks need to be evaluated and steps taken to control them. For example, only the people who absolutely need to know should receive this confidential information and only authorized personnel should be allowed to enter the manufacturing area.

Depreciation

Depreciation rates need to be carefully controlled. Being non-cash expenses, documentation is the key. Assets need to be entered in the right depreciation class so that the correct depreciation rate is applied. The impact on financial statements can span many years if not caught early. Strong financial controls would prevent having to restate several years of financial statements because of significant errors in depreciation expense.

Leasehold Improvements

Errors in recording leasehold improvements can lead to errors on the financial statements. Often, the question is deciding whether the money spent in altering a building is a leasehold improvement that should be capitalized over several periods or whether it should be a current period expense. For example, repairing a window is obviously a current expense. However, if it cannot be repaired, and a new one is installed, the question is whether it is a leasehold improvement, or simply a more expensive repair. The decision about its treatment will affect the income statement and the balance sheet.

Leases

Financial controls need to effectively govern the recording of leases. They may be treated either as capital leases or operating leases. The different treatments will be based on the documentation for each lease. Establishing a good process will prevent errors in the treatment of leases leading to errors on the financial statements.

Goodwill

Goodwill is recorded only when a company acquires another company for more than the net value of its assets. Financial controls need to make sure that the process of establishing the value of the purchased assets works well and that the amount of goodwill is recorded correctly.

Mergers and Acquisitions

The process of supporting mergers and acquisitions requires that strong financial controls be an integral part of mitigating the risk of making the wrong decision. Because these are usually big decisions that have far-reaching effects for the company, both immediate and far into the future, a clear and well-documented process to mitigate the risk of making the wrong decision is essential. The Board should be involved at this level.

Tax Credits

Tax credits can be found on some public company balance sheets. They are listed as assets that provide a future benefit. Good financial controls should make sure that the number is right and listed correctly on the balance sheet. Often companies that are otherwise worthless are bought for the tax credits on their balance sheet. If the listed value of the tax credits on the balance sheet is wrong it affects the purchase price of the company.

Equipment

Financial controls around the purchase, maintenance, depreciation, and disposal of equipment, have to be effective. For example, if a machine used in the manufacturing process is purchased because of its estimated life, and the depreciation expense set accordingly, making a mistake can be expensive and produce errors in the balance sheet (book value of the equipment error) and in the income statement (depreciation expense error).

Prepaid Expenses

Recording prepaid expenses incorrectly will lead to errors on both the balance sheet and the income statement. Good controls, especially the verification of documentation, need to be in place to mitigate that risk.

Recurring Entries

Because the use of automated recurring entries is so prevalent, the process for recording them needs to be examined. Automated recurring entries usually run monthly and yearly. The risk of repeated errors needs to be assessed and good controls should catch programming errors. For example, automated recurring entries for depreciation have to be verified manually so that the outstanding value of the prepaid expense is correctly listed on the balance sheet. Relying only on the computer is not sufficient.

Customer Deposits

Customer deposits should be listed as liabilities. Financial controls need to make sure they are not recorded as customer account payments by mistake. Although this is rarely done intentionally, it is easy for an employee to think of all money coming in as a sale or a payment.

Asset Securitization

Asset securitization means financing specific assets. Financial controls need to ensure that assets that are already pledged as collateral are not pledged again for obtaining financing. For example, inventory from a supplier should not be used to get financing from that supplier if the bank already holds the inventory as collateral for the bank loan, unless the bank agrees.

Marketable Securities

Since marketable securities can change in value often and quickly, keeping track of the changes means controlling the flow of information and making sure it is always recorded at the current market price.

Assets and Expenses

Financial controls should catch errors in recording assets as expenses, and vice versa. For example, IT equipment should be capitalized (treated as an asset) or expensed depending on its useful life as well as on the amount and type of purchase. Good processes for making those decisions should be in place to reduce the risk of an error.

Chapter 12 Summary

• Valuation of assets is an area where there may be opportunities for fraud.

• Companies need policies regarding assets being sold, purchased, or transferred. The policy should be clear, concise, easy to understand, and communicated to everyone in the company.

• The impact of errors involving depreciation rates can be spread over many years if not caught early. Strong financial controls will prevent having to restate several years of financial statements.

• Is something an item that should be capitalized over several periods, or is it a current expense? Sometimes the answer is not clear, but the decision about its treatment will affect the income statement and the balance sheet.

• Asset securitization is an area that needs to be scrutinized carefully. Financial controls need to make sure assets that are already pledged as collateral are not pledged again for obtaining financing without approval.

Bill 198 in Canada

13

Bill 198 and Sarbanes-Oxley

In 2002, Ontario enacted Bill 198 as *"Chapter 22 of the Statutes of Ontario, 2002"* which is sometimes referred to as the *"Budget Measures Act."* It was a measure to re-establish investor confidence in Canadian markets after the Enron debacle subsequent to the introduction of the Sarbanes-Oxley Act of 2002 in the Unites States. It introduces many similar measures. Although it is specifically Ontario legislation, since most Canadian public companies are traded on the Toronto Stock Exchange, it affects public companies right across Canada.

Bill 198 deals with many budgetary issues, but Part XXVI of the Act deals specifically with changes to the Ontario Securities Act.

Material Changes Must Be Reported Immediately

Section 180 requires that public companies promptly report any material changes since their last filing with the OSC to the Ontario Securities Commission (OSC). They must make these changes generally available on their company web site. The purpose of this requirement is to allow investors immediate access to this important information.

Penalties

Section 181 provides that directors and officers of a company that presents misleading or untrue information in any report filed with the OSC, including financial statements, can be fined up to $5 million and sentenced to 5 years in prison.

Administrative penalties of up to $1 million can be assessed by the OSC for each failure to comply with Ontario securities laws (Section 183).

In addition, under Section 183, the OSC can force the company and executives to give back any gains resulting from the breach. When a company has committed this breach, directors and officers are also deemed to have committed the breach. Depending on the seriousness of each offence, the resulting penalty can include a simple reprimand, being asked to resign as director or officer, a fine of up to $1 million, and a prohibition from serving as a director or officer of any public company (Section 184).

Fraud and Market Manipulation

Section 182 specifically prohibits false or misleading representations with the intent to manipulate stock prices and defraud investors.

Investors Can Sue Directors and Officers

Section 185 gives investors the right to sue companies as well as individual directors and officers for damages resulting from issuing misleading documents, including financial statements, making false oral statements, deliberately avoiding finding out what they should have known, or not making timely disclosures.

For each instance, companies can be liable up to the greater of 5% of their market capitalization or $1 million. Directors and officers can be liable for the greater of 50% of their compensation or $25,000. The court will decide how the liability is apportioned among the defendants.

In addition, damages can be awarded to an investor equal to the difference between the average price paid for the stock and the selling price. If the stock has not been sold, the damages would be the difference between the average price paid for the stock and the selling price 10 days after the event. If the defendant can prove that the drop in price was unrelated to the event, they can mitigate or negate their liability for damages.

Time Limits

Actions must be commenced within 3 years of the release date of the document, 3 years after oral misrepresentation was made, and 3 years after a required disclosure was due.

Disclosures

Section 185 says that companies should have disclosure compliance systems that ensure proper and timely disclosures. Section 187 makes the CEO and the CFO responsible for these disclosure systems.

Pro-forma Information

Forward-looking information, such as pro-forma financial statements that use assumptions about future revenue streams, are required by Section 185 to contain precautionary language clearly warning investors that material assumptions are being made. They must not make unreasonable assumptions, and must explain why the basis for those assumptions is reasonable. Companies are allowed to use expert opinions to justify their assumptions, and often do.

Audit Committees

Section 187 requires public companies to appoint

audit committees who must review and certify any documents to be submitted to the OSC.

Internal Controls

Section 187 requires public companies in Ontario to set up and maintain a system of internal controls for financial reporting and asset management. These controls must provide reasonable assurance that management authorizes transactions, financial statements are prepared according to generally accepted accounting principles, and that assets are correctly accounted for (this includes regular inventory counts) and management controls access to them.

In addition, similar to Sarbanes-Oxley, Section 187 requires that CEO's and CFO's certify a report on internal controls that describes the design of the controls and contains an evaluation of the effectiveness of those controls.

Similar Key Provisions

Bill 198 is modelled on the Sarbanes-Oxley Act of 2002. The key provisions borrowed from Sarbanes-Oxley are:

- Certification of the financial statements by the CEO and CFO
- Certification of the report on internal controls by the CEO and CFO

- Personal liability by officers and directors for any misrepresentations or misleading information contained in documents or oral presentations or for lack of proper disclosure
- Increased penalties

Similar Compliance Procedures

The compliance requirements of the Sarbanes-Oxley Act of 2002 exceed those of Bill 198. So far, the SEC has been interpreting the Act as requiring that internal controls must reduce the risk of producing a material misstatement to a "remote chance." Bill 198 asks only for "reasonable assurance." Companies that are Sarbanes-Oxley compliant will also be Bill 198 compliant.

Around The World

Today's multi-national investing community is insisting that Sarbanes-Oxley become the minimum standard worldwide. The UK is drafting legislation similar to Sarbanes-Oxley and Bill 198. Many other countries around the world are talking about doing the same.

Chapter 13 Summary

• In 2002, Ontario enacted Bill 198 as "Chapter 22 of the Statutes of Ontario, 2002." Like the Sarbanes-Oxley Act of 2002, its goal was to re-establish investor confidence in Canadian markets after the Enron debacle in the Unites States. Although it is specifically Ontario legislation, since most Canadian public companies are traded on the Toronto Stock Exchange, it affects public companies right across Canada.

• Bill 198 is very similar to the Sarbanes-Oxley Act. Bill 198 requires that CEO's and CFO's certify a report on internal controls that describes the design of the controls and contains an evaluation of the effectiveness of those controls.

• Part XXVI of the Act deals specifically with changes to the Ontario Securities Act.

• Section 180 requires that public companies promptly report any material changes since their last filing with the OSC to the Ontario Securities Commission (OSC).

• Section 181 makes directors and officers of a company personally liable for any misleading or untrue information in any report filed with the OSC, including financial statements.

• Section 185 gives investors the right to sue companies as well as individual directors and officers for damages.

• The compliance requirements of the Sarbanes-Oxley Act of 2002 exceed those of Bill 198. Companies that are Sarbanes-Oxley compliant will also be Bill 198 compliant.

• Section 187 requires public companies to appoint audit committees who must review and certify any documents to be submitted to the OSC.

Internal Reporting

14

Is it accurate? Are you sure? Can you prove it?

Sarbanes-Oxley is all about making sure. It is about making sure that the numbers are right, it is about making sure that that the CEO and CFO know everything that they ought to know, and it is about making sure that they can prove it.

Internal Reports: Decision Tools

The Sarbanes-Oxley Act of 2002 is intended to ensure that public company financial statements can be relied upon by investors and lenders. Financial statements all start out as internal reports.

Internal reporting is a tool that is relied upon by the Board, Senior Management, and employees to make decisions. Internal reports provide the data that confirms that directives are being followed and that the desired results are being achieved.

Everything a company does should be measured and can be summarized in an internal report. A faulty internal report could have serious repercussions on the company's financial statements. For example, wrong inventory reports can affect the balance sheet and an inaccurate salaries expense can produce errors on the income statement.

A Closer Watch

Sarbanes-Oxley's requirement for reporting on the effectiveness of internal controls means that everything the company does is being watched more closely. Every process must be scrutinized for possible risks of producing a material misstatement on the financial statement, from recording sales to filing taxes. Management and staff get the feeling that everything they do is being watched. They are right.

Additional Focus on Off-Balance-Sheet Transactions

On top of everything else, the Securities and Exchange Commission has said it will keep a close eye on off-balance sheet transactions because of the Enron experience.

As well, the SEC has warned public company management that their financial statements need to include an explanation of the assumptions they used in setting their accounting policies and how they have been applied.

Foreign Company Internal Reporting

Internal reporting of companies that roll up their financial statements into those of their parent public company in the US must undergo documentation and vigorous testing as well. Because CFO's and CEO's must certify the consolidated statements, they are also, by extension, certifying those of their foreign subsidiaries.

The financial controls of US public companies must incorporate the financial controls of their foreign subsidiaries. Often, the company's audit firm will ask a foreign public audit firm to help provide assurance. The foreign subsidiary's financial controls must meet the same Sarbanes-Oxley standards as that of its parent company. This is why many US subsidiaries operating in Canada and other countries need to become Sarbanes-Oxley compliant. Many CFO's and CEO's are asking the subsidiary's executives to provide their own certification. This is referred to as "co-certification." Often companies ask department managers to "co-certify" as well.

Sarbanes-Oxley Compliance Software

There are many companies offering software to help with the compliance process. Most are a simply a series of questions. Although these questions are a good start, they do not necessarily meet all the needs of all companies. There is no "one size fits all" software solution. For example, one of the questions may ask you if there is a material risk in a particular process.

If you answer yes, the software will list it as a material weakness in controls until you find your own solution to mitigating that risk. Unfortunately, it will not give you the answer because the solution will be unique to your company's situation. You will have to figure that one out for yourself. Nothing can replace the experience and intuition of experienced staff.

Dangers of Self-assessment

Most software suppliers recommend using the software to self-assess to a certain extent. There is always a danger of asking employees to self-assess when you are asking them to point out any weaknesses in the processes under their jurisdiction. A third party consultant might be more objective and point out any weaknesses in controls.

On the other hand, compliance software can be a useful tool to coordinate the compliance effort and avoid duplication while making sure some areas are not forgotten. In other words, the value of the software is that it helps you to keep track of what you have covered.

Documentation

A good guideline for the documentation required by Sarbanes-Oxley is that the language should be as easy to understand as possible. There is no standard format required by the Act.

Documentation should list and describe the company's processes, along with the risks associated with each step in those processes, the risk management plans, the implementation of those plans, and feedback on their effectiveness in limiting the risk, and be summarized in the report on internal controls.

Internal Controls to Manage Risk

Under the risk-focused supervision approach, management must identify the most significant risks to the company and then determine whether risk management and internal control systems are in place to identify, measure, monitor, and manage those risks.

Who Approves Reporting?

Controls should require that managers at every level approve internal reports as the information moves up the chain of command. This makes everyone have a stake in the information that is used for decision-making.

Internal Reporting Becomes External Reporting

Public companies must eventually publish their financial statements. The information contained in the financial statements is drawn from internal reports. Financial controls must ensure that the Board and Senior Management approve any numbers before they are published. Part of that approval process, of course, includes the Board's audit committee. In turn, the audit committee will not provide its approval without a blessing from the audit firm.

Need to Report Significant Events

Internal reports that bring to light significant events or information must be reported to the Securities and Exchange Commission and the public immediately. They cannot wait until the next quarterly reporting deadline. Investors must be made aware of this news right away so that they can decide what to do with their shares.

Role of the Auditor - Year End and Ongoing Process

The audit firm and its auditors will also need to independently certify the effectiveness of the company's internal controls. This may sound like a duplication of work, but it is intended to provide investors and lenders a level of assurance that the controls actually work.

In addition to their traditional role of making sure that the numbers are right, auditors are required by the Act to gather and keep documentation that proves that they have tested the financial controls effectively. They must provide their opinion as to their effectiveness. They must also point out any weaknesses in the financial controls.

Living with Sarbanes-Oxley

The Sarbanes-Oxley Act of 2002 is definitely having an effect.

Companies are carrying the heavy financial burden of becoming Sarbanes-Oxley compliant. The task of documenting the company's processes is a daunting and expensive one. Many smaller public companies are having a hard time coping with the cost of meeting the Act's requirements.

Deadlines are also an issue for many companies because of the lack of skilled personnel to accomplish the task. Experienced Sarbanes-Oxley consultants are in high demand.

For these reasons, there is a growing call for the Securities and Exchange Commission to let up on its mandate to enforce the Act. In other words, they want a break. However, as of this writing, the cry for mercy has gone unheeded and there is little evidence that the SEC is about to relax how it interprets the requirements of the Sarbanes-Oley Act of 2002. So it looks like we will be living with these requirements far into the future.

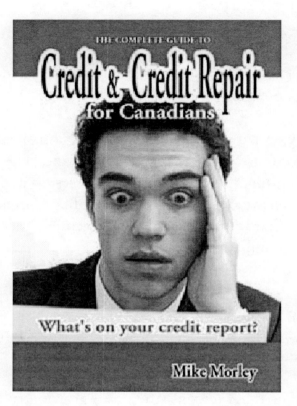

THE COMPLETE GUIDE TO
Credit & Credit Repair
for Canadians

What's on your credit report?

Mike Morley

The Complete Guide to Credit & Credit Repair for Canadians provides step-by-step instructions to enable anyone to fix their own credit report, avoid credit repair scams, improve their credit score, handle annoying collection calls, negotiate with creditors, re-establish credit, get loans approved, and protect themselves from Identity Theft.

Written by CPA and Certified Credit Executive **Mike Morley,** *The Complete Guide to Credit & Credit Repair for Canadians* uses clear, easy-to-understand language to guide people who are looking for ways to recover from a financial setback, put their plan for financial freedom on the fast track, or simply understand how the Canadian credit industry works.

ISBN 0-9737470-0-5

About the Author

Mike Morley is a Certified Public Accountant (Illinois) who holds the top credit designations in Canada (FCI), the United States (CCE), and the U.K. (MICM). He has more than 25 years experience in credit, collections, and finance.

A consultant, speaker, and author, his books and articles on business and personal finance have been published in Canada, the USA, and Australia.

Mike helps guide companies through the Sarbanes-Oxley implementation process. He also helps companies with cash flow problems get back on track.

Mike can be reached by phone at **416-275-1278**, or by email at **mikemorley@sympatico.ca**.

www.mikemorley.com